THINK. PLAY. ACHIEVE!

Achieve! is a research-based series for young learners. It was designed by Houghton Mifflin Harcourt, a global leader in education serving 60 million students worldwide.

WHY IS THIS BOOK DIFFERENT?

There are hundreds of opportunities to practice skills in 4 key disciplines: math, language arts, science, and social studies.

Activities are based on educational standards that emphasize problem-solving. This leads to higher-order thinking. That's when kids take what they've learned to solve *real-life* problems, or create something new.

Activities are also nested in topics that matter to kids: animals, Mars, and fruit smoothies. Achieve! looks like a magazine, not school work. World-class photography makes pages FIZZ.

NOW SAY SOMETHING ABOUT ME!

Oh, yes. This is Cosmo. He's on hand (and he has five of them) to help.

Cover and Front Matter *cover:* owl ©Shutterstock; *inside front cover:* umbrella ©Getty Images; *inside back cover:* NASA patch ©NASA; *back cover:* antique camera ©Getty Images; 3 owl ©Shutterstock; 4 dog ©Shutterstock; 6 owl ©Getty Images. Chapter 1 9 spider web ©Alamy Images; rabbit ©Getty Images; 11 girl on swing; finger painting; grapes; blue frog; ice skates ©Getty Images; plane ©NASA; 12 mitt ©Corbis; 14 smartphone ©iStockphoto; snail ©Shutterstock; thumbs up ©Getty Images; 15 cobra snake ©Getty Images; 17 peach; stripes ©Alamy Images; crown; bee ©Getty Images; 19 insect ©Getty Images; 20 girl on grass ©Alamy Images; 21 shopping cart ©Getty Images; party hat ©Shutterstock; 22 trumpet ©Corbis; corn; goose; tent ©Getty Images; 23 beach ©Corbis; tube ©Getty Images; 24 owl ©Getty Images; 26 terrier running ©Getty Images; 28 sick girl ©Shutterstock; 30 girl smiling ©Getty Images; mime ©Shutterstock; 31 ship ©Shutterstock; 32 candles ©Superstock; turtle ©Shutterstock. Chapter 2 34 milk ©Alamy Images; apple ©Fotolia; fish ©Getty Images; lettuce ©Superstock; 35 barn ©Getty Images; chicken; cow; horse ©Alamy Images; 38 waterfall ©Getty Images; 39 luggage ©Shutterstock; 40 tree ©Getty Images; bench; slide ©Alamy Images; 41 mouse ©Alamy Images; 42 road markings ©Corbis; license plate ©Getty Images; 43 exit sign ©Corbis; 46 three sunflowers; insect ©Getty Images; 47 mime; present ©Getty Images; 49 dunking basketball ©Corbis; 50 yellow paper ©Shutterstock; 52 rock ©Alamy Images; girls recycling; orange slices; guinea pig ©Getty Images; 53 dogs ©Fotolia; 54 dog ©iStockphoto; kitten; chocolate cake ©Getty Images. Chapter 3 56 basketball; basketball net ©Getty Images; 57 basketball ©Getty Images; 58 crown ©Getty Images; king ©Corbis; 59 ant ©Corbis; 60 cactus ©Getty Images; 61 cactus; scorpion ©Getty Images; 62 dog and cat ©Alamy Images; 65 moose ©Alamy Images; goose ©Shutterstock; 66 rollercoaster ©Alamy Images; goldfish; hot dog; movie popcorn ©Getty Images; 68 blue spoon; cherries ©Alamy Images; mug; candy ©Getty Images; 69 mouse; cheese; mouse ©Getty Images; 70 spaceship ©Getty Images; 71 kids in tree ©Getty Images; 72 sign ©Shutterstock; 73 bee ©Getty Images; 74 toy penguin ©Getty Images; 75 cat; house ©Alamy Images; bicycle; dog bone ©Getty Images; 76 tree house ©Getty Images; 77 dog chewing shoe ©Alamy Images; 79 tractor ©Alamy Images; 80 muffin ©Alamy Images; baby ©Corbis; popcorn; girl jumping; toy truck; blueberries ©Getty Images. Chapter 4 82 clouds ©Shutterstock; 83 girl with scarf ©Getty Images; cat ©Alamy Images; 84 clouds ©Shutterstock; 85 girl with scarf; leaf ©Getty Images; clouds ©Shutterstock; 86 girl with scarf ©Getty Images; 87 clouds with sun ©Shutterstock; 88 clouds ©Shutterstock; 89 clouds with sun ©Shutterstock; 90 dog ©Getty Images; 91 cat ©Alamy Images; 92 goldfish ©Alamy Images; 93 cat; goldfish ©Alamy Images; dog ©Getty Images; 94 grass ©Getty Images; 95 grass ©Getty Images; 96 bow ©Getty Images; 100 mailbox ©Getty Images; 101 bird ©Shutterstock; 102 sandwich ©Getty Images; 103 alfalfa; vegetables; radishes ©Getty Images; 104 beans ©Getty Images; 105 beans ©Getty Images; 106 brook ©Corbis. Chapter 5 108 walrus book ©Shutterstock; walrus on snow ©Cutcaster; 109 alley; tree in field ©Shutterstock; key ©Getty Images; 110 paper bag ©Getty Images; cat ©Shutterstock; 111 boy in window ©Alamy Images; 112 apple ©Getty Images; 114 shark fin ©Getty Images; 115 airplane; pyramid ©Fotolia; 116 walrus ©Corbis; 118 yellow flower; yellow flower petals ©Getty Images; bicycle ©Shutterstock; 119 helmet; purple flower; pink flower ©Getty Images; red helmet ©Alamy Images; 120 polar bears ©Getty Images; 121 Mars ©Corbis; 122 frogs ©Getty Images; 124 ostrich ©Alamy Images; 126 books with apple ©Getty Images; 127 swing sign ©Getty Images; 128 herd of elephants ©Fotolia; 129 elephant ©Corbis; herd of elephants ©Fotolia; elephants drinking ©Getty Images; 130 tornado alley diagram ©Getty Images; 131 sunflower ©Getty Images; 132 lion cub; lion ©Getty Images; 133 stack of books ©Shutterstock; 134 koala ©Alamy Images; trees on savannah ©Getty Images; 135 birds flying ©Alamy Images; King Tut's burial mask; toilet paper ©Getty Images; 136 elephants in field ©Fotolia; 137 elephants in field ©Fotolia; cheetahs ©Getty Images. Chapter 6 140 jarred fruit ©Alamy Images; strawberries ©Fotolia; blackberries; raspberries; boysenberries; blueberries ©Getty Images; empty jars ©iStockPhoto; 141 blue mug ©Getty Images; 144 lemon ©Getty Images; 145 lemon ©Getty Images; 146 galaxy ©Shutterstock; 147 boys in woods ©Getty Images; 150 meadow; squirrel ©Shutterstock; 152 cheese slices ©Getty Images; 154 peach ©Alamy Images; strawberry; mango; pineapple ©Getty Images; 155 giraffe; snake ©Alamy Images; leopard; frog; Dalmatian ©Getty Images. Chapter 7 158 banana ©Corbis; gorilla ©Fotolia; gorillas ©Alamy Images; 161 pebbles; purple pink rock; green rock ©Shutterstock; 163 marbles ©Getty Images; 168 top secret; folder ©Fotolia; 169 top secret; folder ©Fotolia; 171 white dog ©Getty Images; 172 cowboy hat ©Getty Images; 186 stars ©NASA. Chapter 8 193 strawberry ©Getty Images; 194 cactus; toy cow ©Getty Images; binoculars ©Corbis; 195 shark; rubber duck ©Getty Images; 197 clock ©Getty Images; 198 magician ©Corbis; 199 magician's hat ©Getty Images; 202 insect; grass ©Shutterstock. Chapter 9 204 open window ©Getty Images; bedroom ©Photolibrary; table ©Corbis; 205 zucchini ©Corbis; 206 paper clips ©Alamy Images; paper ©Shutterstock; 207 lunch box; paper clips ©Alamy Images; 208 paper clips; bat ©Alamy Images; 209 giraffe ©Alamy Images; squirrel; girl and growth chart ©Getty Images; 210 wood ©Getty Images; 211 wood; jalapeno peppers; rabbit ©Getty Images; 212 tape measure ©Getty Images; 214 fish vendor ©Getty Images; 215 dessert with cherry ©Getty Images; 216 corn ©Corbis; 218 candy; lollipops; large lollipops ©Getty Images; 219 coins ©Shutterstock; 220 coins ©Shutterstock; 223 2 girls ©Getty Images; 224 parchment ©Shutterstock; painted Egyptian stucco ©Fotolia; 225 parchment ©Shutterstock. Chapter 10 228 toilet paper ©Getty Images; 229 sponges ©Getty Images; 230 robot ©Getty Images; 233 tennis ball; shuttlecock ©Getty Images; grass ©Shutterstock; 235 gray mouse ©Corbis; 236 horse ©Alamy Images; 238 gift ©Corbis. Chapter 11 238 bee; gray collared peccary; spider; dragonfly ©Shutterstock; girl jumping ©Getty Images; 239 purple crab ©Alamy Images; coral reef; starfish; butterfly ©Getty Images; read leaf ©Shutterstock; 240 beach ball; magnifying glass; tape measure ©Getty Images; 241 mango ©Getty Images; peach ©Alamy Images; 242 gray mouse ©Corbis; apple ©Getty Images; wildcat; coins ©Shutterstock; 243 large milk carton ©Alamy Images; 244 thermometer ©Getty Images; winter hat ©Alamy Images; 245 dog ear patent; music instrument patent; dog jacket patent ©U;S; Patent and Trademark Office; 246 fossils ©Shutterstock; 248 beakers ©Shutterstock. Chapter 12 250 butterfly ©Cutcaster; blue fish; monkey; red bird ©Getty Images; green snake ©Shutterstock; frog ©Superstock; 251 bird on flower; turtle; frog; scuba diver ©Getty Images; 252 groundhog; cat; water bottle ©Shutterstock; fish; television ©Getty Images; 253 chair; dog at bowl ©Getty Images; scuba diver ©Alamy Images; 254 bee ©Shutterstock; goldfish ©Alamy Images; 255 frogs; tadpole ©Shutterstock; 256 hen; butterfly ©Alamy Images; chicks; caterpillar; goats ©Getty Images; 258 Venus flytrap ©Corbis; fly ©Shutterstock; spider ©Getty Images; 259 fly ©Shutterstock; spider; planter ©Getty Images; 260 beach ©Shutterstock; flower buds; coconut; apple core ©Getty Images; 261 owl; ladybug on flower ©Alamy Images; panda ©Getty Images; squirrel; green leaf ©Shutterstock; 262 man at computer ©Getty Images; cacti; camel ©Shutterstock; penguin ©Corbis; 263 grasshopper; skunk; yellow flowers ©Getty Images; 264 old fashioned telephone; rock; fossils ©Getty Images; 265 old mug; dirty baseball ©Getty Images; insects ©iStockphoto; fossils ©Shutterstock; 266 grass ©Corbis; bird; green snake; grasshopper ©Getty Images; sun shining ©Shutterstock. Chapter 13 268 collapsed building; car in lake ©Corbis; arid landscape ©Fotolia; desert rock formation; volcano erupting ©Getty Images; 269 tall trees ©Getty Images; cotton plant; field ©Shutterstock; 270 dining table ©Corbis; meat; radishes; stars; green cauliflower ©iStockphoto; 271 hurricane map ©Getty Images; 272 owl; sledding ©Getty Images; family on beach ©Alamy Images; 273 girl with umbrella; palm trees blowing ©Corbis; owl; windmill ©Getty Images; lake scene ©Shutterstock; 274 clouds ©Fotolia; clouds ©Corbis; 275 waves; clouds ©Getty Images; clouds ©Corbis; 276 planet ©Getty Images; 277 planet ©Getty Images; 279 eagle on patch ©NASA; 280 galaxy ©Getty Images. Chapter 14 282 sand ©Shutterstock; bucket with tools ©Getty Images; 283 red shovel; tube; beach ball ©Getty Images; 285 ice cream; snowflakes; fire; gold bar ©Getty Images; 286 dog ©Shutterstock; 287 two boys; girl on drums ©Alamy Images; fire alarm ©Getty Images; 288 magnet; screw; safety pin; hat ©Getty Images; two pennies ©Shutterstock. Chapter 15 290 girl in costume ©Getty Images; 291 girl in costume ©Getty Images; 292 rabbit ©Getty Images; 293 gray cat; cactus; kitten ©Getty Images; 294 red car ©Getty Images; 295 jeans ©Shutterstock; 296 galaxy ©Getty Images; 297 galaxy ©Getty Images; 298 tractor ©Alamy Images; 302 maracas ©Fotolia; piñata ©Getty Images. Chapter 16 305 gorilla ©Getty Images; 306 factory line; man on car ©Corbis; teacher with students; baker ©Getty Images; boy at dentist; boy with thumbs up ©Shutterstock; 307 tire ©Alamy Images; red car ©Getty Images; evergreen tree; oranges ©Shutterstock; 308 boy studying ©Getty Images.

ISBN: 9780544372511

hmhbooks.com

Manufactured in the United States of America

DOO 10 9 8 7 6 5 4 3 2 1

4500799746

ACHIEVE!

Edited by Sharon Emerson and Meredith Phillips

Houghton Mifflin Harcourt

Boston   New York

Contents

Phonics

LONG and Short

Sam and Kate want the words below. Say each word. Does it have a **short vowel**? Give it to Sam. Does it have a **long vowel**? Give it to Kate.

cube	pen	dip	hat	eve
lime	lot	mole	cup	tape

Sam

Kate

short vowels

long vowels

A **long vowel** sounds like the name of the vowel, as in K_a_te. A **short vowel** sound does not, as in S_a_m.

The GREAT DIVIDE

Rabbit likes to count **syllables** with his foot. Count with him! Say the word. **Write the number of syllables.**

napkin ___

cobweb ___

sunflower ___

watermelon ___

basket ___

A **syllable** is a chunk, or a beat, of a word. Touch your chin when you say words. It drops once for each syllable!

Goodnight, Words!

Soft **c** and **g** words sleep on the soft pillow.
Hard **c** and **g** words sleep on the hard rock.
Draw a line from each word to its bed.

cake

mice

camp

city

garden

gate

giant

gym

Cent has a **soft c**. Car has a **hard c**.
Gem has a **soft g**. Goat has a **hard g**.

10

Lost and Found

These words lost their **starting** or **final blends. Write the missing blend for each word.** Use the blends in the lost and found bin.

_____ og

_____ ane

_____ ing

_____ apes

_____ ove

_____ ate

ri _____

ha _____

la _____

sw- gl- gr- fr- pl- -ng sk- -nd -mp

My <u>gr</u>andma won a <u>tr</u>ophy at the <u>Bl</u>ending Bee! She beat Saul shri<u>mp</u>!

Double It!

Write the word for each picture. Double one of the letters shown to spell it right!

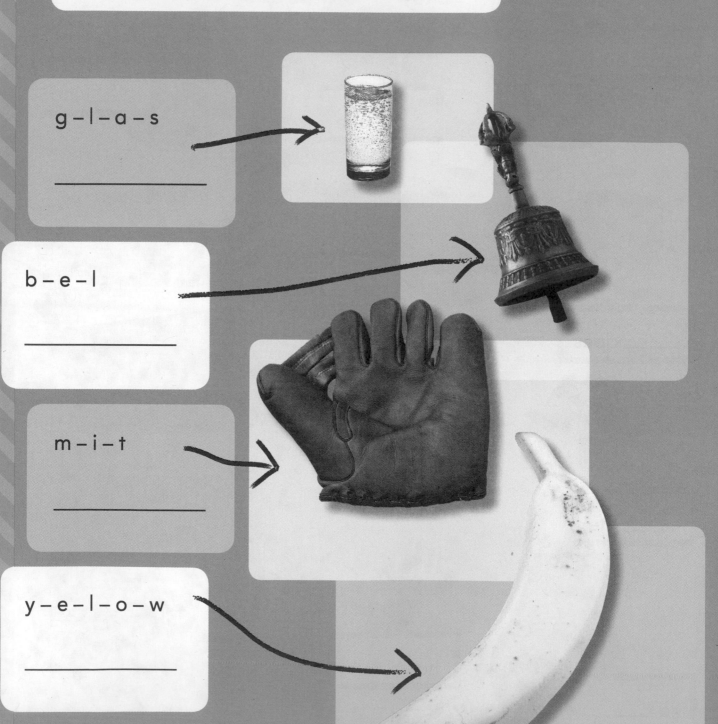

g – l – a – s

_____

b – e – l

_____

m – i – t

_____

y – e – l – o – w

_____

 # Stack It!

Complete the word for each picture.

Does it end with –ck? Then add the word to the stack.

so ___ ___

 The –ck stack

1. _____

2. _____

3. _____

te ___ ___

ro ___ ___

du ___ ___

do ___ ___

All Together NOW!

Some consonants sti<u>ck</u> toge<u>th</u>er to make one sound. These letter combos are called digraphs. Say the word for each picture. **Then draw a line to the digraph in each word.**

ph   sh   th   wh

The **sh** in <u>sh</u>rimp is a **consonant digraph**. You can't hear separate **s** and **h** sounds. If you did, it might sound like *sa-ha*-rimp. And <u>th</u>at's <u>wr</u>ong.

14

PICKY LOLA!

Lola the cobra only eats words that begin with the **CV syllable pattern.**

pilot

sunset

later

favor

mitten

hotel

tiger

Circle the first syllable in each word. Does the first syllable have **one consonant** followed by **one vowel? Then write an L for Lola!**

helmet

Lola looks hungry. Does anyone have a donut?

MAY Words

Celebrate the **long a** in M<u>a</u>y! Say each word. Does it make the **long a** sound? Circle it! If not, cross it out.

MAY

S	M	T	W	T	F	S
pail		car				day
			may		nose	
lime		send				play
				flag		
wait		hail				

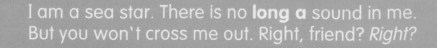

I am a sea star. There is no **long a** sound in me. But you won't cross me out. Right, friend? *Right?*

Beach QUEEN

Read the story below. **Write the missing words.**

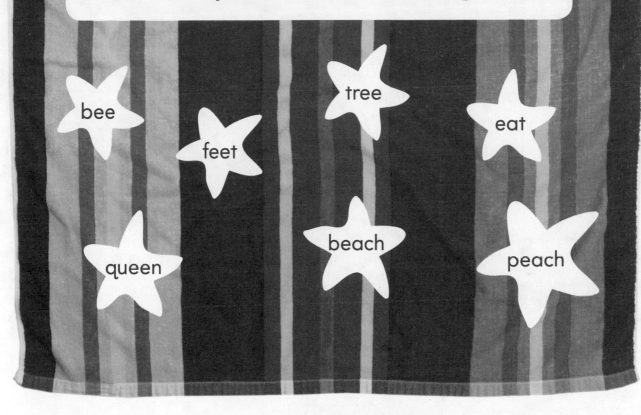

bee

feet

tree

eat

queen

beach

peach

The  _____ is happy. She is going to the _____.

She will _____ a _____ and sit under a

 _____. *Oh, no!* The _____ stung her

 _____.

Sometimes the long **e** sound is spelled **ee**, as in qu<u>ee</u>n. Sometimes it is spelled **ea** as in b<u>ea</u>ch.

Sky HIGH!

Say each word.

Does it have a **long i** sound? Write it on a **long i** step. Does it have a **long o** sound? Write it on a **long o** step.

_____
long i

_____
long o

_____
long i

Start climbing!

_____
long o

_____
long i

coast   find   glow   my
night   pie   zero

_____
long o

_____
long i

18

shy Schwa

dragonfly

o   y

ladybug

a   u

centipede

i   e

Sometimes vowels sound l<u>ou</u>d and cl<u>ea</u>r. Other times they only make an "uh" sound. **Circle the letter under each word that makes the "uh" or schwa sound.**

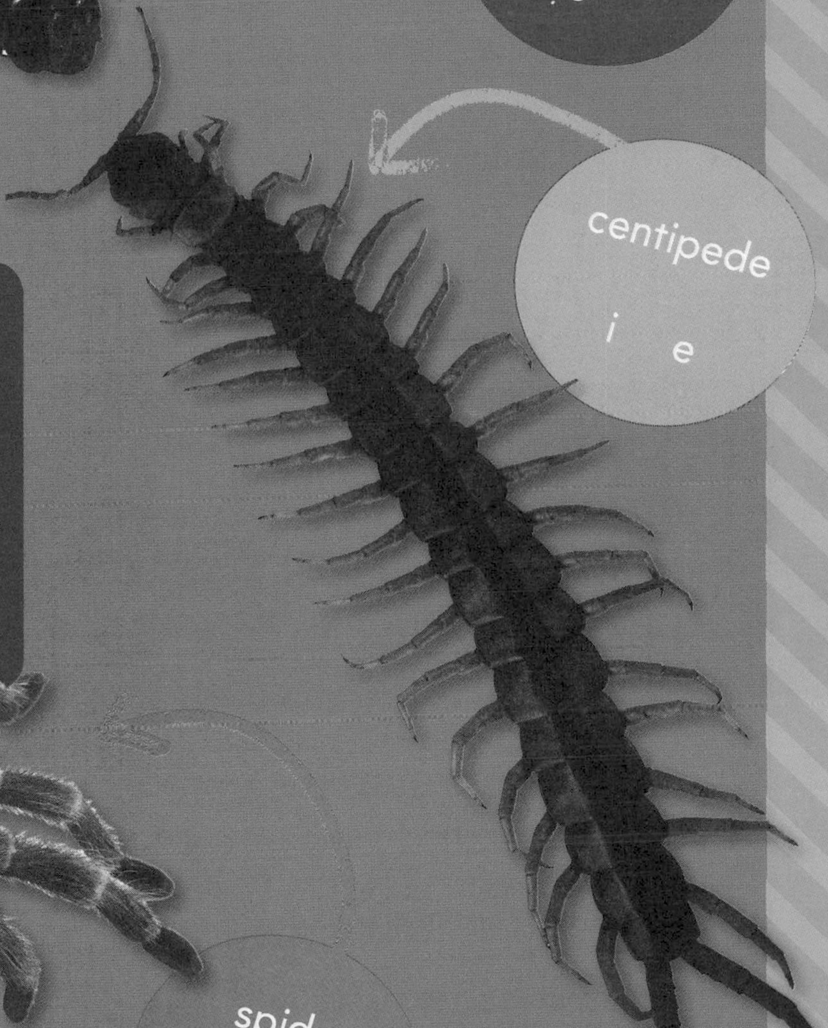

spider

i   e

Are you busy?
Can you help me move my sof<u>a</u>?

A Silly Story

It is _____. Sami sits outside. Sami wants a
(hailing / sunny)

_____ to play with. She will call it _____.
(puppy / robot)   (Ed / Larry)

She will scratch its _____. She will wash its
(ears / belly)

_____ paws. It is _____. Sami goes
(muddy / soft)   (windy / hot)

inside. *Surprise, Sami!* There is a box. Sami looks inside. It's a

_____! Sami is _____.
(hamster / bunny)   (happy / excited)

The P<u>ar</u>ty M<u>ar</u>t!

What will you buy for the p<u>ar</u>ty? Draw a line from the c<u>ar</u>t through the **ar** words to the p<u>ar</u>ty.

cart

yam

drum

shark

leotard

art

wand

tummy

latch

rod

party

A sea st<u>ar</u> has an **ar**! I must be going to the party too!

This OR That?

Cory the stork adores words with **or.** Say the name of each picture. Does it make an **or** sound? **Star it for Cory!**

The letters **o-r-e** also make the **or** sound. Snore is an **ore** word. Can you think of one more?

22

Drifters!

The **er** and **ur** sounds have floated away! Write the missing letters in each word. Then draw a line from the word to the correct **er** or **ur** sound.

wat ___ ___

c ___ ___ b

g ___ ___ m

corn ___ ___

t ___ ___ n

Don't Irk the Bird!

Bird likes it when **ir** makes an **ur** sound.
Say each word. **Does it make an ur sound? Circle it! If not, cross it out.**

shirt   tire

stir   girl

dairy   wire   swirl

I am irked when my cousin Gareth finishes my French fries. What irks you?

Dear, Oh Deer!

Say the words in each pair. They sound the same!
Underline the letters that are different **but make the** same sound.

Underline **two** letters.

p<u>ai</u>r	p<u>ea</u>r
weak	week
blew	blue
toe	tow

Underline **three** letters.

road	rode
tail	tale
main	mane
rose	rows

A pair of pears.

Good Dog!

Doug the dog loves to fetch words with the aw sound. Say the words in each group. Circle the word that has an aw sound.

hand

soft   throw

faucet

pale   broke   book   card

lawn

carry

too   water   park

salt

joke

shhh!

We are in the library. We have to be quiet. Letters can be quiet, too. Say each word. **Circle the silent letter in each word.**

QUIET ZONE

knot

crumb

gnat

wrap

knock

climb

comb

When **b** hangs out with **m**, it is quiet as a lamb.
On its own, **b** can be brash, bouncy, and bombastic!

Ac**HOO!**

Some words make S<u>ue</u> sneeze! Circle words that make the **long oo sound. Cross out words that do not.**

lost   peak   lot

moon   clue

chew

poke

flew

scoop   blue

mug

ten

soup   group

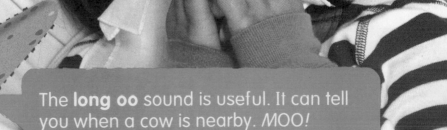

The **long oo** sound is useful. It can tell you when a cow is nearby. *M<u>OO</u>!*

Look again! oo can also make a short oo sound.
Cross out words that make the same sound as look.

foot

hood

bloom

shook

took

room

woof

spoon

brook

A **long oo** rhymes with **boo**. A **short oo** rhymes with **book**. Boo book! Book boo! That sounds like a scary book.

Out On the Town

Complete each word with ow or ou. They sound the same. But only one is right!

cl ___ ___ n

h ___ ___ se

fl ___ ___ er

m ___ ___ th

Ship Ahoy!

Captain R<u>oy</u> is ready to set sail. Finish loading the ship! Circle words that make the same sound as **oy** in b<u>oy</u>. Then draw a line from those words to the ship.

join

boo

noise

hop

coy

boil

enjoy

stop

loop

ploy

Sailors shout *Ahoy!* to get someone's attention. It's like saying, *Hey there!*

Word Turtle

Say the word for each picture. **Write the missing letters.**
Does it end with –le? **Draw a line from the word to the turtle.**

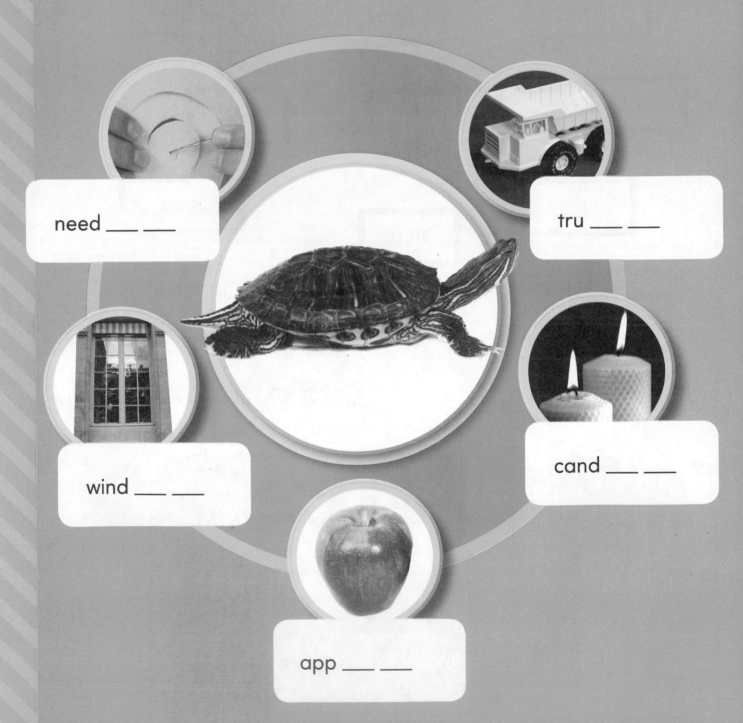

need ___ ___

tru ___ ___

wind ___ ___

cand ___ ___

app ___ ___

Spelling
and
Vocabulary

Shopping List

It's time to go shopping. **List these foods in alphabetical order.**

milk

yams

carrots

pasta

fish

apple

lettuce

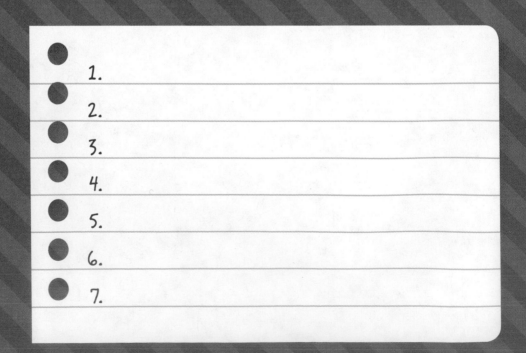

1.

2.

3.

4.

5.

6.

7.

At the FARM

Can you name everything at the farm?
Unscramble the letters.

arnb

___ ___ ___ ___

roseh

___ ___ ___ ___ ___

hccenki

___ ___ ___ ___ ___ ___ ___

corratt

___ ___ ___ ___ ___ ___ ___

wco

___ ___ ___

GET to the ROOT!

A **root** can be a small word inside of a big word.
Circle the root in each word.

retake

prejudge

misread

reading

undone

Which two words have the
same root? **Connect them.**

MAKE a WORD

The prefix **mis-** means to do something *the wrong way*.
The prefix **pre-** means to do something *before others*.

Read the definition.
Then add mis- or pre- to the front of each word.

I heat my food **ahead** of time. I _pre_ heat my food.

I behave in a **bad** way. I _____**behave**.

I match a sock with the **wrong** sock. I _____**match** my socks.

I pay money **ahead** of time. I _____**pay**.

I step in the **wrong** way. I _____**step**.

I look at something **ahead** of time. I _____**view** it.

Spelling and Vocabulary

37

OVERflow WITH OVER

The prefix **over-** is at the front of many words.
Draw a line from each **word** to its meaning.

I am overjoyed.	There are too many people!
I overpay.	It is past the due date.
It's overcrowded!	I use too much.
It is overdue.	I pay too much.
I overuse.	I feel very happy.

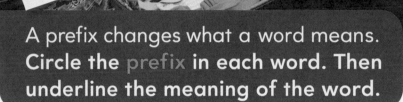

UNpack IT!

A prefix changes what a word means. **Circle the prefix in each word. Then underline the meaning of the word.**

refold

fold again / stretch out

untie

tie again / loosen the tie

repin

put the pin in again / take out the pin

unlock

lock again / open the lock

I like to pack for a trip. Once I packed five toys and five socks. My mom made me **un**pack and **re**pack. I had to *undo* it, then do it *again*.

Spelling and Vocabulary

PaRK CAPeR

Letters are missing from words at the park.

Add the missing letters to solve the case.

tr ___ ___

___ ___ nch

___ ___ ___ des

___ ___ ___ d

___ ___ ___ tue

A MESSY ENDING

Moss is messy! He messed up the ending of these words.
Add -y, -ly, or -ful to the end of each word.

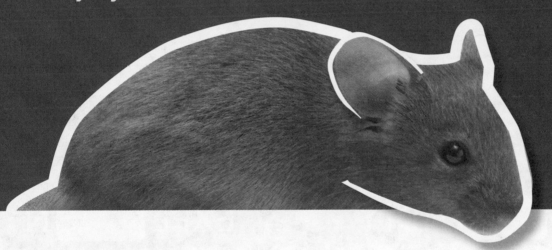

The wind is strong.	It is windly.	It is wind _____.
I do it in a quick way.	I do it quickful.	I do it quick _____.
I am full of help.	I am helply.	I am help _____.
I do it in a slow way.	I do it slowy.	I do it slow _____.
It is full of dust.	It is dustful.	It is dust _____.
I am full of care when I do something.	I am carey.	I am care _____.

Highw_y Five

Kai plays a car game with his brother. They look for cars with words on the license plates. **Write the missing vowels on each plate.**

a   ai   i   igh

K [ ] NDLY

EXPL [ ] N

FR [ ] TEN

T [ ] STED

REW [ ] ND

EXIT 92

INTERSTATE 64 EAST

Louisville

Are we there yet? **Write the missing letters on each sign.**

o   oa   ow   ee   ea

s [ ] psuds
5 miles

f [ ] lded
9 miles

st [ ] pest
20 miles

r [ ] son
45 miles

bl [ ] ing
50 miles

COMPOUND IT!

Combine two words to make a new word.

Circle the word that can be added to the first word to make a new word.

Write the new word.

after + bow   noon   stairs = _____

play + side   corn   ground = _____

sail + boat   flake   cut = _____

home + ball   work   shine = _____

in + fish   side   room = _____

air + shore   one   port = _____

Starfish is a compound word. It's made up of two smaller words! Can you name them?

SCHOOL TIME

Find eight school supplies below. Some words may be backwards!

```
L Z B S R O S S I C S
V I X H P U E S A G W
X R C E H B L V H L T
E E N N P A P E R U C
V D O X E N V G R E M
Q L F M O P Z Y H P S
O O F Y L K D U B Y W
S F A F S C K M W T G
C R A X B Q Q P X U H
C O Q O L A D V M U K
```

Sounds the Same!

Circle the correct word to complete each sentence.
Then write the word in the puzzle.

Down

1. That is a pretty _____. (flour/flower)

2. I _____ what you said. (heard/herd)

3. She _____ the apple? (ate/eight)

4. Please _____ it down. (right/write)

Across

5. The _____ is nice today. (weather/whether)

6. He felt _____ after running. (weak/week)

7. They _____ a boat. (road/rowed)

8. The _____ ran in the woods. (dear/deer)

Homophones are words that sound the same but are spelled differently.

TAKE TWO!

Gabby wants two of everything. Each word below is a **homograph**. It has two meanings. **Draw a line from the homograph to its two meanings.**

slip
- slide easily
- a small piece of paper
- very strong

present
- to move away
- not absent
- a gift

ring
- jewelry for a finger
- a large plant
- a circle

second
- a painting
- part of a minute
- right after the first

Homographs are words that are spelled the same but mean different things. Sometimes they are pronounced differently. You put a *bow* on a gift. You take a *bow* after playing Hamlet.

STOP and GO

Choose a word in the box. Write it below. Then find the word that means the opposite. Keep going until you use all of the words in the box.

ANTONYMS

find	below	yell
above	fill	weak
lose	whisper	empty
	strong	

___stop___ and ___go___ are antonyms!

___find___ and _____

_____ and _____

_____ and _____

_____ and _____

_____ and _____

Put Them TOGETHER

Draw a line to connect words that mean the same thing. These are **synonyms**.

leap	sleepy
little	happy
glad	infant
brag	jump
baby	small
tired	boast

My favorite hobbies are snacking and eating. *Hmm*. That might be one hobby.

Dear GRANDPOP!

Alex typed a letter to her grandpop. **Circle spelling mistakes. Draw a line from each misspelled word to its correct spelling.**

build   decided   by   sprinkles

Dear Grandpop,

Summer is alredy here! I decited to bild a fort. I will finish it bye the time you vist. Than we can make cupcakes with sprinkels. We will eat them in the fort. I look forword to seeing you!

Love,
Alex

Then   forward   visit   already

All SORTS of WORDS

Oops! The buckets tipped over.
The words fell onto the floor.
Can you put them back?
Write each word on the correct bucket.

PLACES

_____

_____

_____

JOBS

_____

_____

_____

TOOLS

_____

_____

_____

airport

hammer

chef

museum

paintbrush

rake

library

teacher

doctor

It's THIS & THAT

Write two words to describe each picture.

hard   juicy   caring   helpful   gray

tasty   small   cuddly

_____
_____

_____
_____

_____
_____

_____
_____

My mom says
I am juicy, soft,
and cuddly.
She is so caring.

SAY What You MEAN!

It's a sunny day. But how does it *feel*? Circle the **strongest** word. Underline the **weakest** word.

hot   scorching   warm

Complete each sentence with the best word.

It's a cool day. The meerkats feel _____ in the sun.

The meerkats return underground. The tunnel protects them from the _____ African sun.

A PLAY On Words

It's raining cats and dogs! That means it's raining very hard. Look at the underlined **idiom** in each sentence. **Write the meaning that can replace it.**

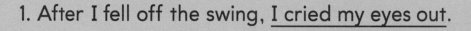

understands something well

stay cheerful   cried a lot

hurry up   do your best

1. After I fell off the swing, <u>I cried my eyes out</u>.

_____

2. If we do not <u>shake a leg</u>, we will miss the bus.

_____

3. He has done that many times and <u>knows the ropes</u>.

_____

4. You should always <u>put your best foot forward</u> at school.

_____

5. Try to <u>keep your chin up</u> even when something sad happens.

_____

"It's a piece of cake!" can mean "it's easy!" I prefer when it means that there is a piece of cake. *Chocolate* cake!

Grammar
and
Mechanics

Shoot the Ball!

Draw a line from each ball to the correct net. *Swoosh.*

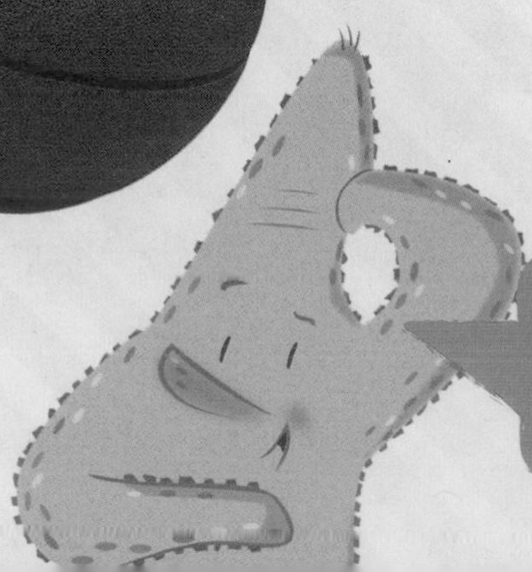

nouns

ant

girl

pour

sit

verbs

song

walk

A **noun** is the name of a person, place, or thing. A **verb** is an action word.

56

boldly

happy

adjectives

nicely

quietly

solid

adverbs

young

An **adjective** describes a noun. As in, throw the *small* ball! An **adverb** describes a verb. As in, *quickly* throw the ball! Many adverbs end in **–ly**.

The KING'S SUBJECTS

The **crown** is the king's favorite **subject**. Help the king find all his subjects. **Underline the subject in each sentence.**

The bird flew away.

The throne broke.

The princess learns math.

The moat was cold.

Ollie visits the castle.

The **subject** tells *who* or *what* did something. To find it, first look for the verb. Then ask *who* or *what* did it?

Where Is the Action?

Andy the ant likes to be where the action is. Help him find the action. **Underline the predicate in each sentence.**

Everyone went inside.

Jane read the book.

The cat woke up.

Tim wore a hat.

The tree fell down.

A sentence has two parts – a subject and a predicate. The **predicate** always has a verb. It *tells what the subject did.*

A Sentence for Stan

Some of these are sentences. **Add a period to sentences.** They have a subject and a verb. **Cross out ones that are not.** Stan the scorpion will pinch those!

Stan lives in the desert

The size of a teacup

Pick a small

It burrows in soil

Eats insects

One kind of sentence does not have a subject – a **command**. That's because the subject is *YOU*. When your mom says *Go to bed!* you can guess that she wants *YOU* to go to bed.

Stan learns that there are different kinds of sentences. **Draw a line from each sentence to the kind of sentence it is.**

The desert is hot.   • command

Is the desert hot?   • exclamation

Find some shade.   • statement

Stan needs shade now!   • question

A **statement** tells something. A **question** asks something. A **command** gives an order. An **exclamation** has a strong feeling. It's my favorite kind of sentence!

JOIN FORCES

Tango and Cat do everything together. The subjects in these sentences want to join forces too. **Write a new sentence for each pair.** Use and to join the subjects.

Aldo ran in the race. Felix ran in the race.

Aldo and Felix ran the race.

Cara fed the cats. Kelly fed the cats.

_____

Tara ate dinner. Tom ate dinner.

_____

Justin made the bed. Amelia made the bed.

_____

Sentence Scramble

These sentences are scrambled. **Put the words in the correct order to make a sentence.**

book she the liked

horse a lives farm on the

goes lake the path around a

Start each sentence with a capital letter.
End it with a period.

Pick Teams

Joe and Beth pick teams. Read each sentence. Is it a simple sentence? Draw a line to Joe. Is it a compound sentence? Draw a line to Beth.

The birds chirped all morning.

Bill went to the store, and he bought a shirt.

Everyone ate the apples, but no one ate the oranges.

We should go inside, or we might get cold.

Tia likes to read books.

The cat and dog played together.

A **compound sentence** is made up of shorter sentences joined by *and, but,* or *or*.

What Did They Say?

Moose and Goose meet on the street. Add **quotation marks** to the words they **say out loud.**

I am a majestic creature, says Moose.

I am majestic, too, says Goose.

Moose asks, What makes you majestic?

Goose says, I can spread my wings wide!

Hmm. That is majestic, says Moose.

The goose asks, What can you do with your wings?

These are not wings. These are antlers, says Moose.

Oh, says Goose.

My cousin Gareth told me a secret. He said, "Don't repeat what I say." *Oops.* I just told you what he said.

Three or More

Each sentence has a **series** of nouns. Some commas are missing. **Separate the nouns with commas.**

Nina Joe and Suzy went to the amusement park.

They ate hot dogs popcorn, and pretzels.

Mom Dad, Vi and Rex rode the roller coaster.

Rex won a goldfish a ball and a unicorn.

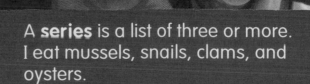

A **series** is a list of three or more. I eat mussels, snails, clams, and oysters.

66

More Commas, PLEASE!

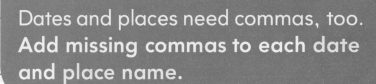

Dates and places need commas, too. Add missing commas to each date and place name.

Sara moved on March 2 2009.

She moved to Miami Florida.

Luke got a dog on November 17 2013.

He got the dog in Cleveland Ohio.

My grandparents got married on June 23 1970.

They got married in Phoenix Arizona.

A sea star is born! My nephew Gil was born on April 2, 2014. He lives off the coast of Wilmington, North Carolina.

MORE than ONE!

David goes to the art exhibit. **Write a name for each artwork.**
It should tell the **number** and **name of objects** in the picture.

marble

spoon

five marbles

_____

cherry

mug

_____

_____

To make a noun plural, you usually just add –s. If the
noun ends in *ch*, *x*, *sh*, or *s*, you add –**es**. If it ends in a
consonant + *y*, you change the *y* to **i** and add –**es**.

One Mouse, Many Mice

singular noun

↓

child

man

woman

person

foot

goose

tooth

ox

The plural names of some nouns are irregular. **Draw a line from each noun to its plural.**

irregular plural noun

↓

women

feet

people

oxen

teeth

children

men

geese

Those **mice** have nice **feet**!

Past, Present, and Future

Pack the cars for a road trip. Draw a line from the verb to the right car.

turned	will turn	turn
stay	stayed	will stay
will jump	jump	jumped

past tense

future tense

present tense

A **past tense** verb *happened* in the past. A **present tense** verb *happens* now. A **future tense** verb *will happen* later.

Let's Agree!

Del and Waldo agree. Circle the verb that **agrees**, or sounds best, with each subject.

Kyle (play / plays) ball every day.

The doctors (walk / walks) to the operating room.

The players (run / runs) around the court before every game.

My sister (listen / listens) to music after school.

Becky (put / puts) the toys away.

His parents (drive / drives) him to school.

Sometimes we add an **–s** to a noun to make it plural. It's the opposite with verbs. One dog play**s**. Two dogs play.

Rule Breakers!

NO RULES APPLY

Some verbs break the rules. They are irregular! **Circle the** irregular past tense **of each verb.**

Today I...	Yesterday I...
feel	feeled / felt
hide	hid / hided
eat	ate / eated
get	getted / got
drive	drived / drove
say	said / sayed
break	breaked / broke

It figures. Irregular verbs use an irregular verb to **break** the rules! The past tense of **break** is **broke**!

Bart's Be Hive

Bart built a hive for his favorite verb.
Use Bart's **be** hive to complete the chart.

Bart _____ smart!

be

present
am   are   is

past
was   were

Subject	Present	Past
I		
You		were
He, She, It	is	
They	are	

A Proper Postcard

Poppy the penguin is proper. Cousin Pippy is not! Pippy sent a postcard to Poppy. She forgot to capitalize **proper nouns**. **Circle each letter that should be capitalized.**

march 8, 2014

Dear Poppy,

Is it cold in antarctica? It is warm here! I am in miami, florida. My hotel is on the beach. I can see the atlantic ocean from my window. The football team is called the dolphins. They should change it to the penguins! I swim home on tuesday. See you soon.

Your cousin,

pippy

To: poppy

antarctica

From: pippy

florida

A **proper noun** is the actual name of a person, place, or thing. Have we met *properly*? I am Cosmo.

It Belongs to...

Do not eat that bone! It is Donny's bone. The things in these sentences also belong to someone. **Complete each sentence.**

This is _____ _____.
   Mike

_____ _____ is playful.
   Omar

Her _____ _____ is on Main Street.
   friend

Add **'s** to the end of a noun to make it possessive. This is *my oyster*. This is *Cosmo's oyster*!

Psst! It's a Pronoun!

Do you know the secret password to enter Mindy's tree house? It's a **pronoun**! **Cross out the underlined noun. Write a pronoun above it.**

She
~~Mindy~~ is inside the tree house.

Mindy's friends visit the tree house every day.

The tree house is made of wood.

Mindy's dad built it.

A **pronoun** can take the place of a noun. Some pronouns are **she**, **he**, and **it. They** are also passwords to Mindy's tree house!

Yours and Mine, His and Hers

Do not chew Myrna's toy! It is (hers.) Who owns the things in each sentence below? **Circle the possessive pronoun.**

The book is yours.

That sweater is mine.

My bus is always on time.

Your painting is pretty.

Her grandparents live in Texas.

His cat is outside.

The desk is hers.

The folder is his.

My, your, his, and **her** show up before a noun. **Mine, yours, his,** and **hers** usually show up at the end of a sentence.

Shorten It!

Maximillian the macaw has a long name. Call him **Max** for short. You can shorten these words too. **Draw a line from each word to its abbreviation.**

January	Rd.
Avenue	hr.
hour	Mon.
Street	Jan.
Monday	Nov.
Road	min.
November	Ave.
minute	St.

Titles can be abbreviated. When I become a doctor, you can call me Dr. Cosmo.

Pushy Words

Use an apostrophe to push words together. It's easy! **Write the words in each** contraction.

contractions with *not*

don't = ___ + not

isn't = ___ + not

won't = ___ + not

aren't = ___ + not

contractions with *pronouns*

I'm = _____ + am

they're = _____ + are

it's = _____ + is

we're = _____ + are

A **contraction** can also be one shortened word. You can push the letters together in **cannot** to make **can't**.

The Bluest Activity!

Compare the pictures!

Circle the **crunchiest** snack.

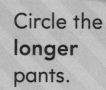

Circle the **longer** pants.

Circle the **younger** child.

Circle the **softest** toy.

Reading

The Contest

by Mia Lewis

Sun and Wind were talking.

"I'm stronger than you," said Wind. "I can blow a ship across the sea. I can bend a tree to the ground."

"I'm stronger!" said Sun. "I light the day. I can dry up that stream!"

This story has two main characters. Write their names. **Draw a picture of each character.**

Name: _____   Name: _____

Sun saw a boy on the road.

"That boy is wearing a coat," said Sun. "We will have a contest. If you can make the boy take off his coat, you are stronger. If I can make him take it off, I am stronger. You go first!"

Draw a line to the correct answer.

What does Sun want to do?

talk to the boy
rise in the sky
have a contest

Why?

to stop the boy
to prove who is stronger
to learn something new

Wind agreed. He wasted no time. He blew a swift breeze at the boy. The traveler did not notice.

Wind blew a stronger gust. The boy held onto his hat. He kept walking.

Complete each sentence.

1. Wind _____ to the contest.

2. Wind blew a breeze that was _____.

3. The gust Wind blew was _____ than the breeze.

4. The boy does not let go of his _____.

Find your answers in the puzzle.
Some words may be backwards.

```
S D R P Z D E T G
T W C N E G T E M
D C I E G B I D S
B E R F G T G H D
L G B B T H A T H
A V V J P B Q L I
R E G N O R T S X
A T E D B P D F I
T C L N S T U Q A
```

Now Wind blew a real storm! The trees shook!
Leaves were flung into the air.

Wind blew as hard as he could. The boy only
pulled his coat more tightly around himself.

What word tells what the <u>trees</u> did? _____

What word tells what the <u>leaves</u> did? _____

What word tells how the <u>boy pulled his coat</u> around
himself? _____

Look for the underlined words in the story. That's where you'll find the answers!

At last Wind gave up. "You try," he said to Sun. "Good luck!"

Sun smiled. He shone a little ray. The boy kept on walking.

"You see," said Wind. "Neither of us can get him to take off his coat."

Cross out the false statement.

Wind wins the contest.

Sun smiles.

Why do you think Sun smiles?

_____

_____

_____

Sun was not finished. He shone another ray on the boy. He beat down hot and steady.

The boy began to sweat. He took off his hat. He opened his coat. After a while, he took his coat all the way off.

Why did the boy sweat? Circle the sentence that tells the **cause**.

What other **effects** did Sun have? Circle them.

The boy took off his hat.

The boy walked faster.

The boy opened his coat.

Circle the **cause** in each pair.

It rains.   I wear rain boots.

I eat pizza.   I am hungry.

I go to bed.   I am tired.

A **cause** always happens before the **effect**. It tells you why something happens.

Wind clapped. Sun bowed. The boy walked peacefully down the road in his T-shirt.

The story has a moral. *Persuade gently*. It works better than force.

How do you know that Sun won the contest? Underline a sentence.

Write the moral of the story in your own words.

_____

_____

_____

_____

_____

A **fable** is a story that has a **moral**. It teaches a lesson!

Number the events in the order they happen in the story.
This will help you remember it!

[ ] Sun and Wind agree to have a contest.

[ ] Sun wins the contest.

[ ] Sun and Wind argue over who is stronger.

[ ] Sun sees a boy on the road.

[ ] Wind blows on the boy.

[ ] Sun shines on the boy.

You can be a storyteller! Tell this story to someone else.

The BEST Pet

by Judy Rosenbaum

Are you looking for a pet?

A dog is a fine pet. A dog will play with you. It can be a pal.

A dog can be a big job, though. You have to walk it. You must brush its coat. A dog can eat a lot, too.

Dogs won't always do the right thing. Some dogs chew everything. Dogs can be loud. Some dogs like to run off.

A dog can be a big job. Circle one reason.

It will play with you.   It needs to be walked.   It can be a pal.

A dog is like you! Sometimes it may not do the right thing. Circle one thing.

It can be loud.   It can eat a lot.   It will play with you.

You could get a cat. Cats are fine pets. They love to jump, climb, and play.

A cat can be a big job, though. You must brush its fur. You must feed it. You don't have to walk a cat, but you need to spend time with it.

Cats won't always do the right thing. Some cats scratch tables and chairs. Some cats hide and spring out at you. Many cats like to be up at night. They might make noise while you are trying to sleep.

Do these describe a dog, a cat, or both? Add them to the diagram.

need brushing   need walks   may be loud   may hide

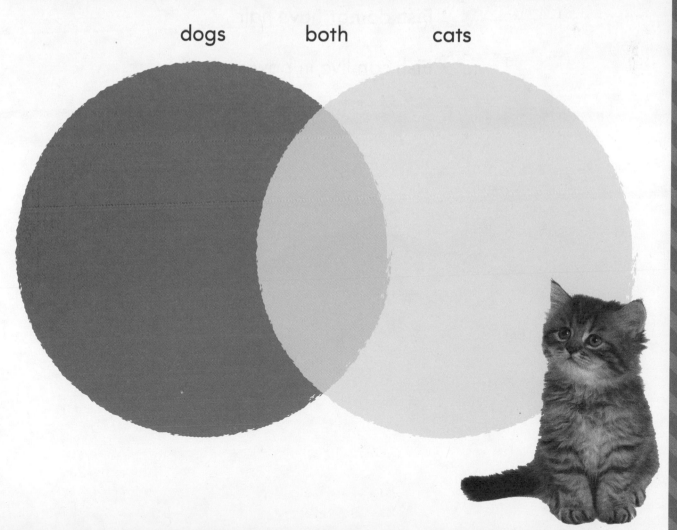

dogs   both   cats

What if you want a quiet pet? Then don't look just at mammals. Think about fish!

Fish make no noise at all. They don't get out of the house and run off. They don't scratch things. They don't even have paws!

Fish are not hairy like dogs or cats. So you don't have to brush them. They don't need to be walked. Fish are easy to care for. You just have to clean the bowl.

What can you tell about **fish** by looking at this picture?

○ Fish are quiet.

○ Fish do not have paws.

○ Fish do not have hair.

○ Fish can live in bowls.

Write **two details** about each animal.

dog _____

_____

cat _____

_____

meow

fish _____

_____

Which is the best pet for you? A dog, a cat, or a fish? Or perhaps something else?

I want a _____ .

BEST Friends

by Margaret Maugenest

Mai and Jenny were best friends.
They lived next door to each other.

A tree stood between their homes.
It had a straight trunk. The top of the
tree looked like curly green hair.

Draw a picture of the tree
between two homes.

Jenny and Mai wrote notes to each other. They put the notes in a tree. It was their secret hiding place.

It was Jenny's birthday. Mai got Jenny a present. She wrote Jenny a note.

Add a "secret hiding place" to the tree trunk.

Complete the sentences.

Mai got Jenny a _____ because it was Jenny's _____.

Mai also wrote Jenny a _____.

Draw a line to the text that describes this picture.

The note said to come to Mai's house.
Mai put a red bow around the note.
She put it in the tree. Then she waited.

Jenny did not come. Mai checked the tree.
Her note was gone.

What happened to the note? **Circle one.**

I think that

the note fell out of the tree.

Jenny took the note from the tree.

a squirrel stole the note.

Mai looked at Jenny's house. She saw kids. They lined up in a row. They had presents. They went into Jenny's house.

Jenny was having a birthday party! Why didn't she invite Mai?

Draw of a picture of Mai.
Show how you think Mai feels.

Write one word telling how you think Mai feels. _____

Why do you think Mai feels this way?

_____

_____

_____

Mai sat on her swing. She felt mad.

Jenny came. "Why aren't you at my party?" she said.

Mai got off the swing. She stood tall. "You didn't invite me!" she said.

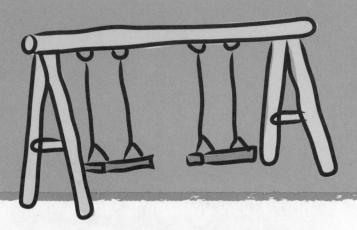

Rewrite what Jenny and Mai said to each other in the speech bubbles.

Show what you learned from the dialogue by completing these sentences.

Jenny wants _____ to be at her party.

Mai thinks she was not invited to the _____.

"I DID invite you. I put a note in the tree," said Jenny.

The girls heard a noise. They looked up. They saw a bird in a nest. The nest had paper. It had a red bow.

What do Mai and Jenny see on the nest? _____

Draw what Mai and Jenny see on the picture of the nest.

"That bird took our notes. It took the ribbon. It used them for its nest!" said Mai.

Jenny and Mai still write notes to each other. Now they put their notes in a box. They are still best friends.

Circle the paragraph that tells the problem Mai and Jenny had.

Underline the sentence that tells how they solved their problem.

Did you ever have a **problem**? Did you find a **solution**? I bet that's a good story!

The bird wants more paper for her nest! Explain why there is no more paper. **Tell her the beginning, middle, and end of the story.**

Draw a line to connect each section to its action.

beginning

middle

end

Jenny and Mai see that the bird took their notes. They decide to put their notes in a box.

Mai gets Jenny a birthday present. Mai puts a note for Jenny in the tree.

Jenny does not visit Mai. Mai sees that Jenny is having a party. Mai gets upset. She thinks she was not invited.

Growing Sprouts

by Mia Lewis

Do you eat sprouts? Maybe you **eat** them on sandwiches. Maybe you eat them in salads. They are used in cooked food, too.

This sandwich has a lot of sprouts.

Draw a salad with sprouts. **Write** a caption below it.

Caption: _____

A **caption** tells what is in a picture.

You can buy different kinds of sprouts at a store. Some are mild. Others are spicy. They taste different because they are grown from different kinds of seeds.

mung bean sprouts

alfalfa sprouts

radish sprouts

The **text** *tells* you that there are different kinds of sprouts.

The **photos** *show* you how different kinds of sprouts _____ (circle the best answer).

sound   look   smell

Perhaps the best thing about sprouts is how easy they are to grow. You can grow them at home.

All you need is a cup and some seeds. Put the seeds in the cup, and add water. Soak them overnight.

In the morning, pour off the water. Rinse the seeds twice a day. They will be ready in three to seven days. Sprouts offer good nutrition.

Someone is growing sprouts!

Why do you think the author wrote this text? **Circle one.**

a. She wants people to stop growing flowers.

b. She wants people to try to grow sprouts.

c. She wants people to read more books.

Underline the sentence on this page that supports your answer.

Complete the directions for growing sprouts.

Step 1: Put _____ in a cup.

Step 2: Add _____ .

Step 3: _____ them overnight.

Step 4: The next morning, _____ off the water.

Step 5: Rinse the seeds _____ a day.

If you grew sprouts, how would you eat them?

_____

_____

_____

By the STREAM

I took my little paper boat
And put it in the stream.
The boat was bobbing up and down.
I fell into a dream.

I sailed the mighty Rio Grande.
For Big Ben, I was bound.
The rushing water got quite swift.
The boat was flung around.

I dreamed it ran into a rock
And sank into the deep.
But all was well, and so I fell
Back peacefully to sleep.

Circle the true statement in each set.

The poet sailed the Rio Grande.
The poet dreamed about sailing the Rio Grande.

The paper boat ran into a rock.
The poet dreamed the paper boat ran into a rock.

Some poems **rhyme**. Can you find the words
that *rhyme*? Look at the end of every *line*!

Writing

WHICH is WHICH?

Wally the walrus wants to be a writer. Teach him the basics. **Draw a line from the** name of the writing part **to an** example.

sentence

A walrus is a marine mammal. Walruses have long tusks. They live mostly near the Arctic Circle.

paragraph

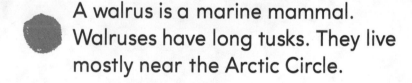

book

 A walrus is a marine mammal.

A Terrific Title

Circle the best title for each book.

a book about tornadoes

Tornado Time!

Our Earth

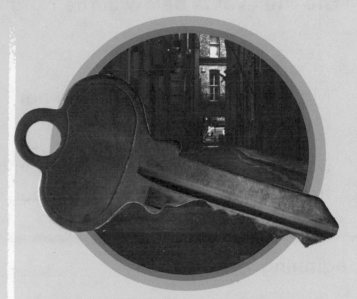

a book about a girl who solves a mystery about a lost key

The Case of the Missing Key

That Key Is Mine

a book about how to plant a tree

Write a title for this book.

_____

_____

I am writing a book. It's called *Diary of a Sea Star*. Can you guess what it's about?

Molly and Her Cat

This story is scrambled. Can you fix it?
Write the events below in the right order.

Her cat jumped out of the bag!

Molly was worried. She could not find her cat.

Molly heard a crackling noise coming from a bag. She looked in the bag.

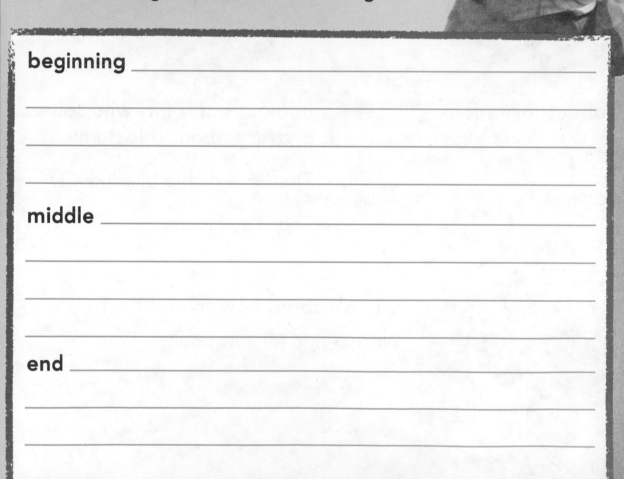

beginning _____

_____

_____

_____

middle _____

_____

_____

_____

end _____

_____

_____

_____

A story's **beginning** sets up a problem. The **middle** gives details about the problem. The **end** tells how the problem was solved.

Make It Up!

Orin woke up early to play soccer. Use the picture to tell the whole story.

Tell the **problem** Orin has

Give **details** about the problem.
Tell how Orin feels about the problem.

Tell how Orin **solves** his problem.

Write a **title** for your story.

About an Apple

Use the words in the box to describe the apple.

crunchy
juicy
red
smooth
sweet

Smell
_____

See
_____

Hear
_____

Taste
_____

Feel
_____

Write What You Sense!

Julie takes a walk with her family.
Imagine that you are on the walk too!

What do you **hear**?

_____

What do the leaves **feel like**?

_____

What do you **smell**?

_____

Thanks for describing this!
Leaves don't get **crunchy**
under the sea.

See It! Hear It!

fly
squeak
happy
white
bells
wonderful

Imagine you are on a boat. **Describe what you see and hear.** Use words from the box, or use your own words.

Title: _____

When I am on a boat, I see and hear many _____ things. I see waves with _____ crests. I hear _____ on buoys. I see gulls _____ above. I hear dolphins _____. I feel _____ on a boat!

Think of a title for your paragraph. **Write it above.**

114

Tell the
ORDER

Complete the sentences to
tell what happens.

First, Toby _____.

Then, Toby _____.

Finally, Toby _____.

Look at the sentences. Circle the words
that tell the order **things happened.**

A FUN Day

Wally the walrus wrote a story about a fun day. **Underline why it was fun.**

Swimming with My Grandfather

by Wally

One day, I went swimming with my grandfather. First we jumped into the cold water. Then we dove deep into the ocean. We saw a sunken ship! We went inside. There were many clams. So we ate them! Finally we swam back to the surface. It was a fun day!

It's your turn to tell a story. Here are some ideas. Can you think of any more?

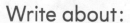

Write about:

The day I got a pet

The day I spent with a favorite relative

The day I went to a fun place, like a park

The day I _____

A story can be made up. A story can be true. A true story about yourself is called a **personal narrative**.

Choose an idea and write about it. Then draw a picture.

_____

by You

_____

_____

_____

_____

_____

_____

_____

_____

ALIKE!

Tell how the two flowers are **alike**.

Both flowers are _____.

Write a sentence telling how the two bicycles are **alike**.

_____

_____

Different!

Tell how the two flowers are **different**.

One flower is _____ , but the other flower is _____ .

Write a sentence telling how the two helmets are **different**.

_____

_____

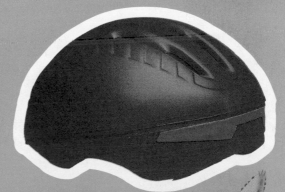

Sometimes two things can be alike **and** different. My great aunt Frida is a sea star. But she has twenty arms!

Polar Bear HOMES

Read the paragraph.

Polar bears live in dens in the far north. They dig the dens out of snow and ice. Their fur helps them stay warm in their cold, snowy homes. Sometimes they build their homes in the middle of a snow bank. Most polar bears dig their dens in the fall. A polar bear's den makes a good home.

The topic sentence is highlighted.
It tells you the main idea. This is about dens.

Underline the sentences with supporting details.
Details tell you more about the main idea – dens!

Circle the closing sentence.
This sentence finishes the paragraph.
It ties the ideas together.

This paragraph informs. It is informatory!

Start Off Strong

Read the paragraph. **Circle the best topic sentence.**

The Planet Mars

Mars is a planet.

Mars is an interesting planet.

Mars is a fun place to visit.

_____ One interesting fact about Mars is that it has a lot of iron oxide. It makes the planet look red. Another interesting fact about Mars is that it has two moons. They are called Phobos and Deimos. Many scientists study Mars. There is nothing boring about Mars!

Details, Details

This paragraph is missing supporting details. **Add** details **to the paragraph.** Look at the pictures for ideas.

Two Different Frogs

The red-eyed tree frog is very different from the green tree frog. One difference is that the red-eyed tree frog has _____, but the green tree frog has _____. Another difference is that the red-eyed tree frog is _____, but the green tree frog is _____. Even though they are different, they are both frogs.

Details give you more information about the main idea. They make it interesting! I have five arms. But here's an interesting detail They are bony! That stops others from eating me.

The BIG Idea

Read the paragraph.

Celebrating Spring

People around the world celebrate spring in different ways. In England, children dance around maypoles. They call the holiday May Day. In Pakistan, boys fly kites on the first day of spring. They call the holiday Basanth. In India, Hindu children throw colored powder into the air. They call the festival Holi. _____

Circle the best closing sentence.

These celebrations are all different, but they all honor spring.

There are many different names for the first day of spring.

The best celebrations, however, take place in the winter.

Ostrich Opinion

Read the paragraph.

The Best Bird

Ostriches are the best kinds of birds. First, they are big! Second, they can run really fast. They have special claws on their feet that look like hooves. The claws help move their feet. Third, they can hear and see very well. Ostriches are different from other kinds of birds and that makes them more interesting.

The topic sentence is highlighted. It tells the writer's opinion.

Underline the sentences with reasons and examples. The writer gives reasons for having this opinion.

Circle the ending sentence. The writer repeats the opinion in different words.

SUPER SATURDAY

What is the best thing to do on Saturday?
Complete this paragraph.

The best thing to do on Saturday is _____.

One reason is that _____. Another

reason is that _____. Finally, I love doing

this because _____. For these reasons,

_____.

Draw the best thing to do on Saturday.

Identify the Parts

Read the persuasive paragraph.

More Homework!

I think teachers should give homework on Fridays. We get homework every other night during the week. Why should Friday be different? First, homework helps us remember what we did in class. Second, there is more time for my family to help me on the weekend. We should all ask to have homework over the weekend.

The **topic sentence** is highlighted.
It tells the writer's opinion.

Underline the sentences with reasons and examples.
The writer gives reasons for having this opinion.

Circle the ending sentence.
The writer says what he wants readers to do.

PERSUADE ME!

Do you want to rebuild the park? **Use** two of these reasons **to complete the paragraph.**

- the benches are all broken
- the gate is brand new
- some of the plastic swings are torn
- the slide is fun to go down

The playground near the public library is in bad shape.

First, _____.

Second, _____.

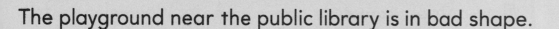

It used to be fun to go to the park, but now no one goes there because it is too old. We need to ask adults to rebuild the park.

Elephant Expert

The Elephant Journal asks you to write about elephants. This is what you write:

Elephants

Introduction —
Elephants live in India and Africa. They are very big. They drink water and communicate in interesting ways.

Body —
Elephants are the world's biggest land mammals. They can weigh more than 6 tons. Some grow to be 12 feet tall. An elephant's trunk can be 7 feet long and can weigh 400 pounds.

An elephant uses its trunk to suck up water. Sometimes it curls its trunk into its mouth to drink the water. Other times it squirts the water over its body to keep cool.

Elephants use sounds to communicate. When elephants are mad, they make a trumpeting sound. When elephants want to say hello to each other, they use low grumbling sounds.

Conclusion —
Elephants are impressive. These large animals do many amazing things.

The journal asks you to underline the main ideas in the body section. There is one main idea for each paragraph.

Pictures can help people understand the main ideas. Draw a line from each **main idea** to the **best picture**.

Elephants are the world's biggest mammals.

Elephants use their trunks to suck up water.

Elephants use sounds to communicate.

A Clear Story!

A map can help people understand a story's main idea. What story can you tell using the map below? **Circle it.**

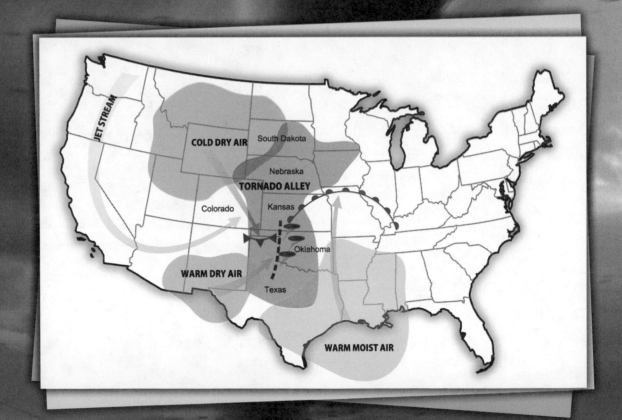

JET STREAM

COLD DRY AIR   South Dakota

Nebraska

TORNADO ALLEY

Colorado   Kansas

Oklahoma

WARM DRY AIR

Texas

WARM MOIST AIR

A tornado is a spinning column of air. It can travel many miles.

Florida has a higher average of tornadoes than most states.

Tornado Alley is the name of an area that has many tornadoes.

Photo: Dan Craggs

Plant Sitter

Who will water your plants when you are away?
Add these steps **to the paragraph below to find the answer.**

1 put the glass of water next to your plant

2 push one end of the rope into the soil

3 put the other end of the rope in the water

_____

Plants need water in order to grow.
Are you going away for a while? You
can still water your plants. You'll need a
thin cotton rope and a glass of water.
First, _____
_____.
Next, _____
_____.
Last, _____
_____.
The water will travel through the rope from the
glass to the plant. So you do not have to worry
about your plants while you are away!

Give your how-to paragraph a title.
Write it above the paragraph.

DON'T Tame It! Label It!

Draw a line from each label to the part on a lion.

- mane
- teeth
- back
- tail
- paw

Lions hang out in a large family called a pride.

Read THIS!

Think of a book you like. **Fill in the blanks to write a book review.**

Book Title: _____

Written by: _____

Reviewed by: _____

This book is about

_____

_____

One reason I liked this book is

_____

_____

Another reason I liked this book is

_____

_____

My favorite character _____
looks like this

That looks like a great book. Please send a copy to Cosmo, Atlantic Ocean.

Prompt Me

A **prompt** asks you to do something. **Look at the sentences.**

Kenya is a country in Africa.

Tell what the climate is like in Kenya.

Write four sentences about the climate in Kenya.

1. Underline the **topic**.

2. Write what you need to **tell** about the topic. (This is a prompt!)

_____

3. Circle how many sentences you need to write.

1 2 3 4

Here's a new topic.
Write a **prompt** for it!

The koala lives most of its life in a eucalyptus tree.

Tell _____
_____.

Write four sentences about
_____.

I use my arms to walk on the sea floor. When I get home, my mom prompts me to wash my arms.

134

Find It Online

Circle the best website to learn more about these topics.

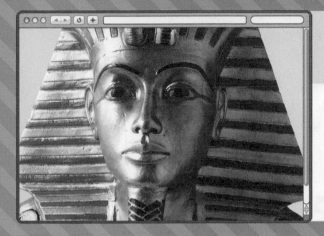

Who discovered King Tut's tomb?

a website about famous discoveries

a website about King Tut

Why do birds fly south in the winter?

a website about winter

a website about birds

How are trees turned into toilet paper?

a website about how toilet paper is made

a website about trees

To learn about me, you can search for "sea star" or "starfish" on the Internet. Or you can search for me at the beach!

Superior

A good way to take notes is to write information in a grid.
Complete this grid with information from the two sources.

Lake Superior	Encyclopedia	Great Lakes Facts
Where is it?		
How big is it?		
Deepest point?		

Encyclopedia

Lake Superior is bordered by Michigan, Wisconsin, Minnesota, and Canada. It has a surface area of 31,700 square miles. At its deepest point, it is 1,333 feet deep.

Great Lakes Facts

Lake Superior is in North America. It is about the size of Maine. It is as deep as 1,333 feet.

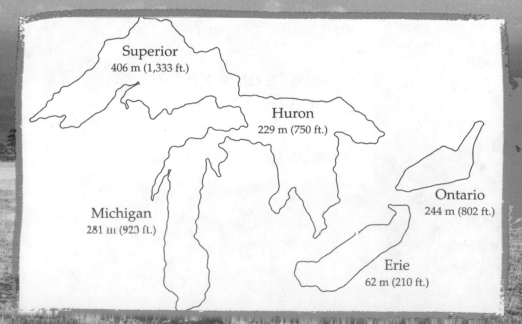

Superior
406 m (1,333 ft.)

Huron
229 m (750 ft.)

Ontario
244 m (802 ft.)

Michigan
281 m (923 ft.)

Erie
62 m (210 ft.)

Color in Lake Superior.

NOTES!

A cheetah is a large cat. Fill in the grid to tell **where it lives**, **how fast it is**, and **how it hunts**.

Cheetah	Websites	Books
where it lives		

Circle the most interesting thing you learned about a cheetah.

Make IT GOOD!

Good writing has six traits.

- ideas supported by reasons and details.
- correct punctuation, grammar, and spelling.
- **Good writing has...**
- your voice!
- interesting words.
- different kinds of sentences.
- a structure that makes sense.

Check the group that uses different kinds of sentences.

_____ Cheetahs are mammals. Cheetahs are the fastest land mammal. Cheetahs can run up to 70 miles per hour. Cheetahs can grow to 4.5 feet long. Cheetahs can weigh up to 140 pounds.

_____ Cheetahs are the fastest land mammals. They can run up to 70 miles per hour. These quick creatures can grow to be 4.5 feet long and can weigh up to 140 pounds.

I have six good traits. I am caring, kind, friendly, polite, honest, and a good dancer.

Number
and
Operations

Berries for Barry

Barry is making fresh berry jam! Add the tens and ones. **Write the total number of berries in each jar.**

1 ten + 5 ones = 15

2 tens + 7 ones =

5 tens + 4 ones =

8 tens + 9 ones =

9 tens + 3 ones =

Some people call shellfish "fruits of the sea." Shellfish jam is my favorite flavor. One jar has 12 shellfish. That is 1 ten and 2 ones.

Planet Sweetopia

It's tea time on Planet Sweetopia. Sweetopians love sweet tea. Draw a line to match stacks of sugar cubes to the right teacup.

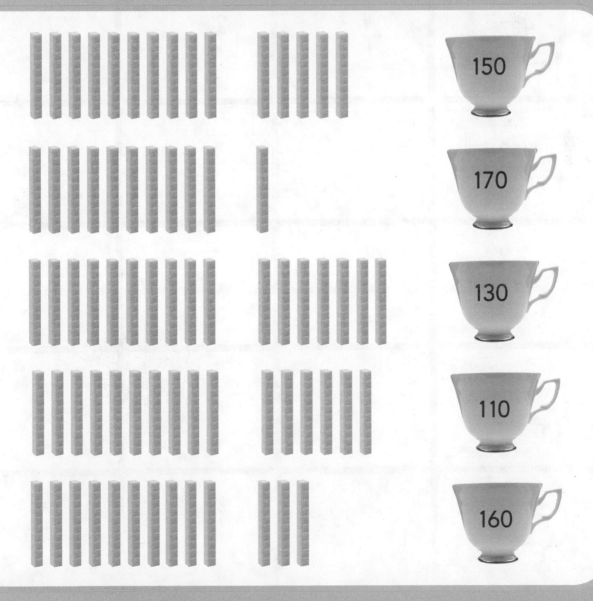

Sheep Counter

Each night, Arlo counts sheep to go to sleep. **Write the number of sheep as hundreds, tens, and ones.**

Number of Sheep	hundreds	tens	ones
437	4	3	7
262			
591			
814			
705			

Cross-Number Puzzle

Use the clues to write a 3-digit number.
Put one digit **in each square.**

Across

1. 3 hundreds 2 tens 3 ones

3. 3 hundreds 7 tens 9 ones

5. 4 hundreds 2 tens 1 ones

Down

2. 2 hundreds 5 tens 3 ones

4. 9 hundreds 2 tens 3 ones

Who's Got

Marisa, Pablo, and Tate play darts. Look at each board. Write the score.

Marisa

hundreds	tens	ones

Score _____

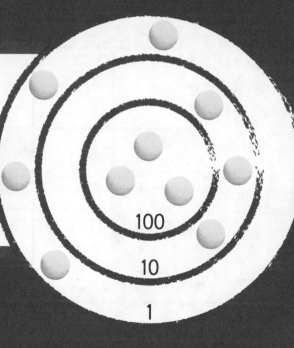

100
10
1

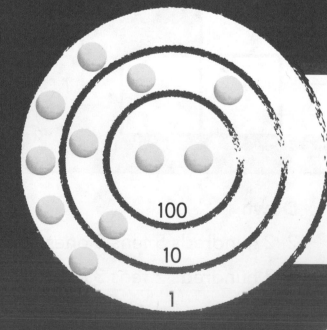

100
10
1

Pablo

hundreds	tens	ones

Score _____

Game?

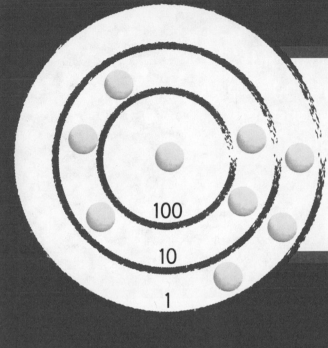

Tate

hundreds	tens	ones

Score _____

Vita joins the game. **Draw the balls on the board to match her score.**

Vita

hundreds	tens	ones
2	3	1

Score _____

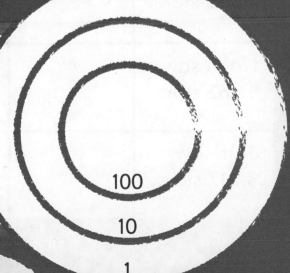

Who won?

_____

Starry Night

Sasha and her friends start a star-gazing club. They see thousands of stars each night. Write the number of stars another way.

	thousands	hundreds	tens	ones
Sasha saw 2,632 stars.	2			
Mia saw 1,945 stars.				
Noah saw 4,163 stars.				
Jett saw 3,217 stars.				

GO GRANOLA!

The Granola Scouts raised money to build a new hike-and-bike trail in their community. **Write the total each raised.**

Noah has 3 thousands
2 hundreds
4 tens
7 ones
He raised = $ _____

Jett has 6 thousands
4 hundreds
1 tens
0 ones
He raised = $ _____

Mia has 2 thousands
9 hundreds
5 tens
8 ones
She raised = $ _____

Sasha has 4 thousands
7 hundreds
3 tens
6 ones
She raised = $ _____

Number and Operations

SECRET NUMBER SOCIETY

Edna created a secret code to write numbers.

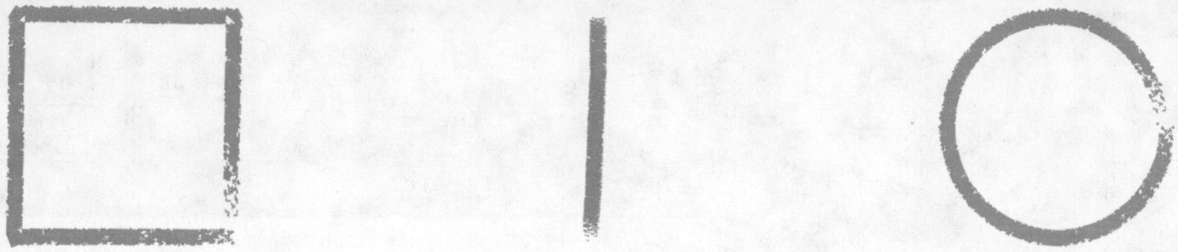

□ | ○

hundreds　　　　**tens**　　　　**ones**

Finish each code below.
Draw the missing hundreds, tens, and ones.

354

□ || □ ○○○○

253

□ ○○○ |||

216

○○○ | ○○

314

□ ○○○○ □

264

|||| ○○○○ □ □ |||

284

□ □ || ○○○○○

Count Skips-a-few

Count Skips-a-few likes to count in different ways.

He counts by **fives**.

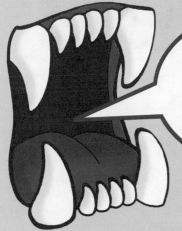

5, 10, 15, 20, 25...

10, 20, 30, 40...

He counts by **tens**.

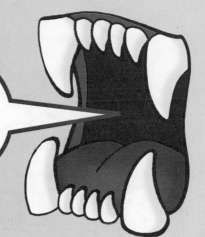

Now it's your turn!

Count by **fives**.

20, 25, 30, ___, ___, ___, ___,

55, 60, 65, ___, ___, ___, ___.

Count by **tens**.

10, 20, _____, _____, _____,

60, 70, _____, _____, _____.

Count by **hundreds**.

100, 200, 300, _____, _____,

600, _____, _____, _____, 1000.

Simon's nuts rolled out of the tree. Help collect them. Start with **214**, the circled acorn. Then count by **10s**. **Circle each acorn in the pattern.**

Aw, Nuts!

157
322
222
214
200
622
153
422
224
101
412
153
143
522
244
234
722
522
183
254
193
274
284
222
264
199
133
294
722
275
506
220
351
304
281
314
453
101
284

150

Dot Surprise!

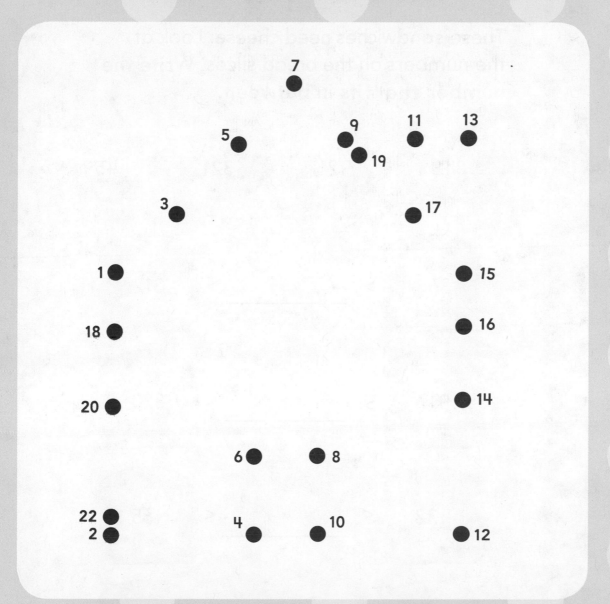

Start at 1. Connect the odd numbers from **least** to **greatest**.
Then start at 2. Connect the even numbers the same way.

Cheese, Please!

These sandwiches need cheese. Look at the numbers on the bread slices. Write the number that fits in between.

843   921   321   459

366 > _____ > 312

917 > _____ > 820

432 < _____ < 465

988 > _____ > 856

Mabel's Marbles

Mabel has an amazing marble collection. Compare the numbers. **Write >, <, or = in the blank circle.**

 459 ◯ 605

blue marbles   red marbles

 719 ◯ 719

green marbles   yellow marbles

 250 ◯ 205

orange marbles   purple marbles

 504 ◯ 405

black marbles   white marbles

I have > arms than you!
You have < arms than me.

Feed the Dragon

Sherman the fruit-eating dragon is starving! Match the words to a number.

152

18

one hundred
eight tens
seven ones

eight hundreds
one ten
nine ones

496

one ten
eight ones

819

three hundreds
two tens
four ones

four hundreds
nine tens
six ones

187

one hundred
five tens
two ones

324

Seeing Spots!

Write the number of spots on each animal.

three hundred, sixteen

_____

two hundred, thirty-two

__232__

two hundred, twenty

_____

ninety-seven

_____

one hundred, fifty-eight

_____

I have five eye spots. They are not like your eyes. I can only see light and dark.

Jellybeans!

How many jellybeans are there? Everyone guessed. Write each **number** using words.

250

_____

98

_____

649

_____

317

_____

Addition
and
Subtraction

GOR(LLAS in the MATH

Add the numbers in each bunch.
Then draw a line to the gorilla with the same sum.

Bunch 1
6 + 2
4 + 4
5 + 3
1 + 7

Bunch 2
4 + 3
5 + 2
2 + 5
1 + 6

Bunch 3
2 + 3
1 + 4
5 + 0
4 + 1

Bunch 4
4 + 5
3 + 6
8 + 1
2 + 7

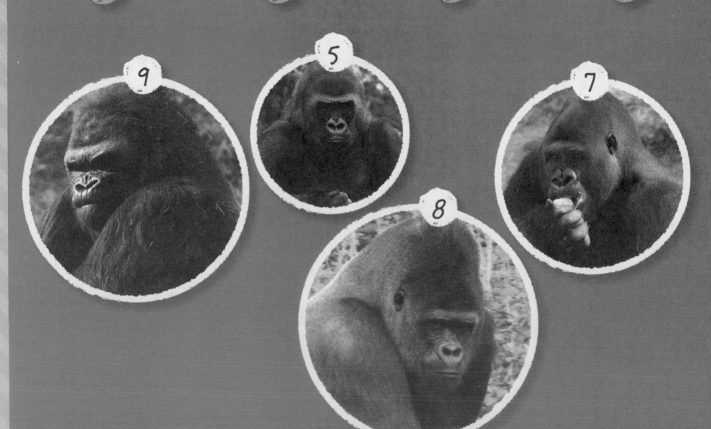

9

5

8

7

DOUBLE Trouble

Practice making doubles. **Add the dots on these dominoes together.**

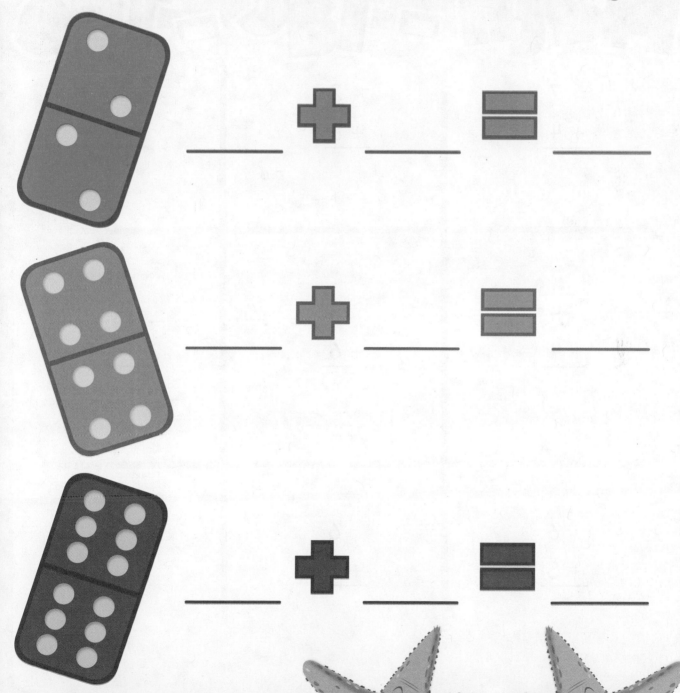

_____ + _____ = _____

_____ + _____ = _____

_____ + _____ = _____

I practiced making a double!
Now how many arms do we have?

159

Solve these problems to win math-tac-toe!
Make an **X** over boxes with the same sums.

Math - Tac - Toe

7 + 4	2 + 8	8 + 1
4 + 4	3 + 6	4 + 5
6 + 3	6 + 2	4 + 7

Tyson's ROCKS

Tyson has 13 rocks.
He puts 8 into one pile.
How many are in the other pile?

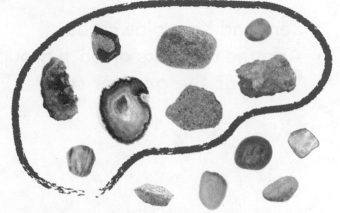

_____8_____ + _____ = 13

Tyson puts 10 into one pile.
Circle 10. Now how many
are in the other pile?

_____10_____ + _____ = 13

Tyson makes 3 piles.
How many are in each pile?
Does Tyson still have the
same number of rocks?

_____ + _____+ _____ = _____

Hearts Are WILD!

Jem and Katy play cards.
Add the numbers on each group of cards.
Who has the greater sum?

Jem has _____ +

_____ + _____ = _____

Katy has _____ +

_____ + _____ = _____

Jem has _____ +

_____ + _____ = _____

Katy has _____ +

_____ + _____ = _____

Marble Madness

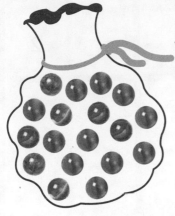

Jen has 7 red marbles and 11 blue marbles.
How many marbles does she have altogether?

_____ marbles

Alexia had 14 marbles.
She gave _____ to Steve.
How many does she have left?

_____ marbles

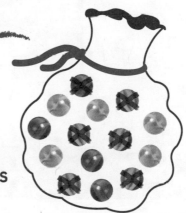

Draw marbles to match the story.

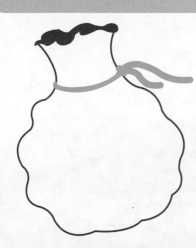

Carter had 13 marbles.
He gave 4 to his brother.
How many marbles does Carter have now?

_____ marbles

Addition and Subtraction

SUM PEOPLE

Solve each puzzle. **Fill in the missing numbers.** The numbers 1, 2, 3, and 4 must be used in each row, column, and square.

Puzzle 1

	2	3	4
	3		
			2
	4		

Puzzle 2

		3	1
			2
3			1
		4	

Puzzle 3

4		2	
	1		
			4
3			2

Puzzle 4

2			
	4	1	
4			
			3

Broken Hearts Club

$17 + 4 = \underline{21}$

$27 + 6 = \underline{}$

$45 + 6 = \underline{}$

$32 + 9 = \underline{}$

$66 + 7 = \underline{}$

$39 + 5 = \underline{}$

$58 + 9 = \underline{}$

$50 + 1 = \underline{}$

$60 + 7 = \underline{}$

$20 + 1 = \underline{21}$

$40 + 4 = \underline{}$

$40 + 1 = \underline{}$

$30 + 3 = \underline{}$

$70 + 3 = \underline{}$

Make a match!
Draw a line to connect
number sentences with
the same sum.

MIX & MATH

58 + 12

56 + 27

67 + 23

29 + 29

43 + 18

32 + 19

Make a puzzle pair.
Draw a line to the matching sum
on the opposite page.

60 + 10

31 + 20

60 + 23

41 + 20

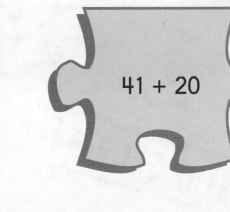

70 + 20

30 + 28

SECRET IDENTITY

Each person has a secret identity!
Write the total number of tens
and ones on each card.
Then write the sum.

**Draw a line to the card
with the matching sum.**

TOP SECRET — Barclay

26 + 26 = _____

_____ tens _____ ones

TOP SECRET — Rain

14 + 47 = _____

_____ tens _____ ones

TOP SECRET — Laszlo

37 + 36 = _____

_____ tens _____ ones

TOP SECRET — Bea

32 + 28 = _____

_____ tens _____ ones

TOP SECRET — Cal

48 + 36 = _____

_____ tens _____ ones

004

43 + 17 = _____

_____ tens _____ ones

001

19 + 33 = _____

_____ tens _____ ones

002

39 + 22 = _____

_____ tens _____ ones

003

25 + 48 = _____

_____ tens _____ ones

005

59 + 25 = _____

_____ tens _____ ones

Around the World

Soma made a special hopscotch court. It's a square!

Subtract across and down to fill in missing numbers.

DOGGY Day School

It's snack time for the pups!
Match each bone to a dog.

45 + 18

38 + 18

19 + 52

17 + 34

26 + 49

51

71

75

63

56

A MAZE OF 30s

Slim Thirty lost his cowboy hat.
Help him find it.
Color in boxes that have a difference of 30, 31, 32.

39 – 7 = _____	34 – 9 = _____	35 – 7 = _____
41 – 9 = _____	38 – 8 = _____	
52 – 8 = _____	38 – 7 = _____	
	38 – 6 = _____	
25 – 8 = _____	40 – 8 = _____	37 – 7 = _____
27 – 6 = _____	28 – 5 = _____	37 – 6 = _____

TARGET Toss

Sunil and Sara toss beanbags. They toss two bags each turn.

13	18
20	5

Sunil's total score was less than 20 points.

Which two numbers did his bags land on? **Circle them.**

56	35
6	79

Sara's total score was less than 50 points.

Which two numbers did her bags land on? **Circle them.**

30	23
10	16

Sunil's total score was greater than 50 points.

Which two numbers did his bags land on? **Circle them.**

54	20
31	62

Sara's total score was greater than 100 points.

Which two numbers did her bags land on? **Circle them.**

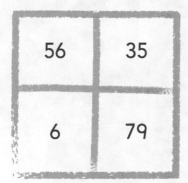

Addition and Subtraction

She Shoots! She Scores!

The Wildcats are on fire!

	Game 1	Game 2
Ramona	18	25
Siobhan	12	13
Terri	19	21
Alexa	15	20

Ramona and Alexa scored
_____ points in Game 1.

Ramona and Siobhan scored
_____ points in Game 2.

Terri scored _____
points altogether.

Siobhan scored _____
points altogether.

Siobhan and Terri scored
_____ points altogether.

Solve each problem. Cross out the squares that have the same answers. Did you get BINGO?

35 – 14 = _____	26 – 14 = _____	35 – 19 = _____	33 – 19 = _____	62 – 36 = _____
29 – 12 = _____	39 – 18 = _____	42 – 19 = _____	64 – 29 = _____	53 – 28 = _____
55 – 16 = _____	43 – 28 = _____	**FREE SPACE**	32 – 19 = _____	53 – 12 = _____
52 – 9 = _____	61 – 25 = _____	41 – 13 = _____	47 – 26 = _____	68 – 39 = _____
57 – 19 = _____	62 – 17 = _____	46 – 28 = _____	54 – 17 = _____	40 – 19 = _____

JIM
APPLESEED

Jim picks 85 apples.

On the way home, Jim gives away apples.
Write how many are left at each stop.

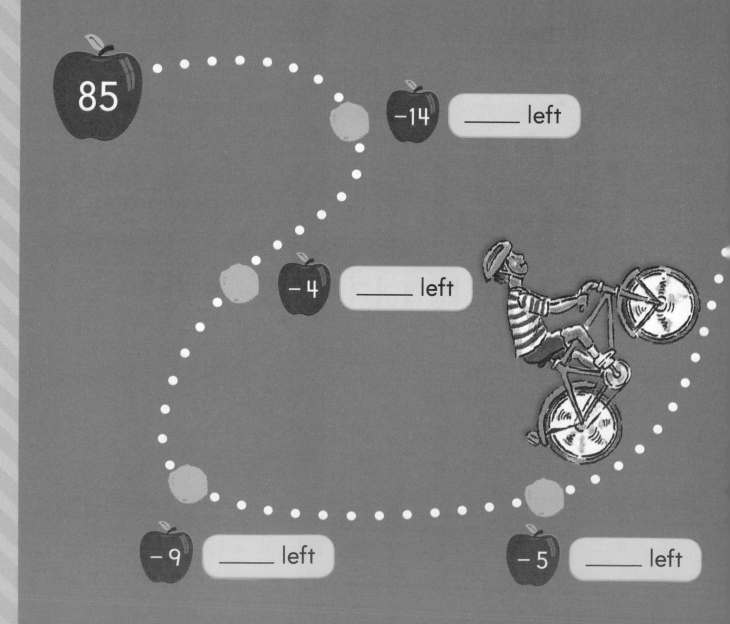

85

−14 _____ left

−4 _____ left

−9 _____ left

−5 _____ left

 − 11   _____ left

 − 7   _____ left

− 6   _____ left

_____ − _____ = 12 left

It's the last stop. Jim wants to keep 12 apples.
How many more can he give away?

Riddle

Solve each problem.
Then write the matching letter below.

A 21

B 32

C 9

D 11

E 40

J 10

K 23

L 51

M 28

R 50

S 14

T 1

U 34

What is a room no one can enter?

50	44	28	38	75	50	38	54
−22	−10	−14	−36	−25	−21	−9	−26

○ ○ ○ ○ ○ ○ ○ ○

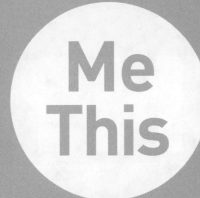

Me This

What falls in winter but never gets hurt?

21	44	38	63
−7	−18	−9	−11

○ ○ ○ ○

F **49**   G **17**   H **2**   I **16**

N **26**   O **29**   P **71**   Q **65**

V **18**   W **52**   X **44**   Y **47**

What has a mouth but can never eat?

67	28	57	60	59
−17	−12	−39	−20	−9

Z **8**

○ ○ ○ ○ ○

What's the PROBLEM?

Someone found the answer! But what is the problem?
Choose numbers to complete the problem.

| 8 | 5 | 16 | 15 |

Emilia made a necklace.

She added _____ blue beads.

She added _____ red beads.

How many beads does Emilia's necklace have? __24__ beads

Tim has more baseball cards than hockey cards.

He has _____ baseball cards.
He has _____ hockey cards.

How many cards does Tim have altogether? __20__ cards

| 20 | 28 | 10 | 4 |

Alex and Sophie played ping pong.

Alex had _____ points.

Sophie had _____ points.

Sophie beat Alex by __10__ points

Terrell painted a picture of Mars.
He used more red paint than brown paint.

He used _____ tubes of red paint.

He used _____ tubes of brown paint.

Tim used __32__ tubes of paint.

BIG Jellyfish

Jellyfish like big numbers. They travel in big numbers. And they subtract in big numbers.

```
  774
- 236
_____
```

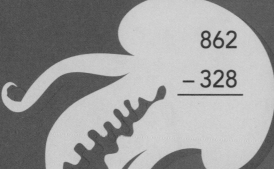

```
  862
- 328
_____
```

```
  772
- 254
_____
```

```
  489
- 273
_____
```

```
  551
- 113
_____
```

$$448 - 363$$

$$679 - 261$$

$$639 - 472$$

$$727 - 256$$

$$967 - 153$$

Some jellyfish glow. They have a built-in flashlight!

BIG TOP

Clowns solve big problems under the big top.
Add or subtract.

375
+ 364

364
+ 419

816
– 345

157
+ 771

942
– 163

801
− 375

523
+ 174

796
− 468

278
+ 465

693
− 241

Lost in SPACE

These subtraction problems are missing numbers. Can you put them back where they belong?

1, 3, 4, 9, 5, 2, 8

Tens	Ones
4	8
− 1	☐
3	4

Tens	Ones
2 / 3	15 / 5
− 1	☐
1	6

Tens	Ones
7	8
− ☐	6
2	2

Tens	Ones
☐ 4	18 / 8
− ☐	9
2	9

Tens	Ones
4	☐
− 1	1
3	1

Tens	Ones
2	8
− 1	☐
1	0

Multiplication

What Are the Odds?

Count the marbles in each group. Circle groups with an **even** number. Draw a square around groups with an **odd** number.

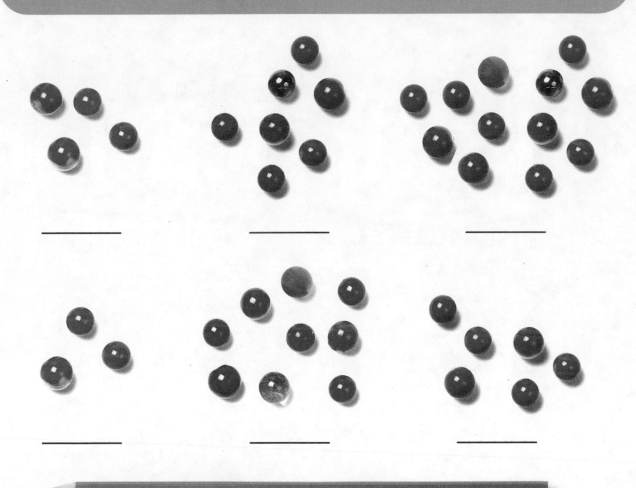

_____   _____   _____

_____   _____   _____

Draw an odd number of marbles.

Jack's Stacks

Jack the grocer puts fruits and vegetables in equal rows.

Jack makes **3 rows of tomatoes**. There are **5 in each row**. **Draw a picture.**

_____

_____

_____

Jack makes **6 rows of oranges**. There are **3 in each row**.

_____

_____

_____

_____

Jack has **25 avocados**. Put them in **5 equal rows**.

_____

_____

_____

_____

Dino Math!

Look at the number.
Draw a line through the same number of dinosaurs.
Then circle **odd** or **even**.

15

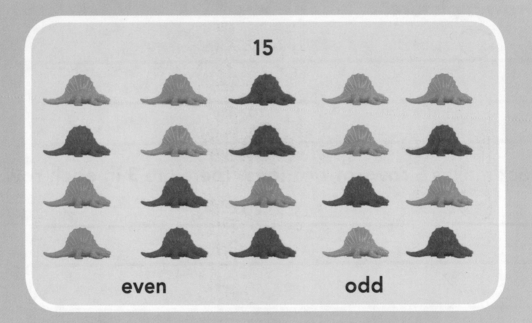

even   odd

18

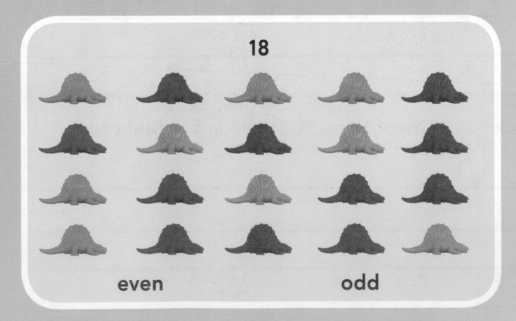

even   odd

13

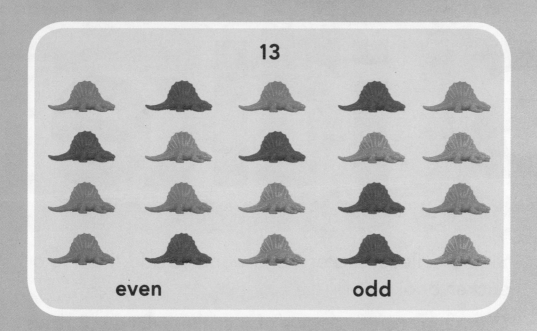

even   odd

20

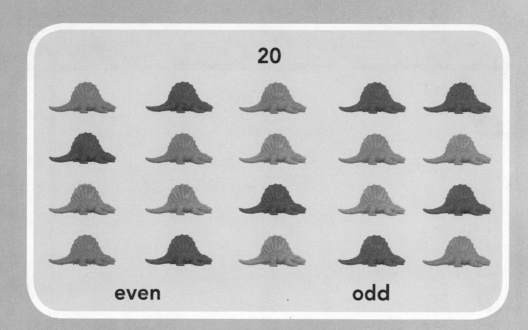

even   odd

If the number is even, you can always make 2 equal groups.

_____ = _____ + _____

Sticker

Stacia collects stickers. She wants to add them to a sticker book.

One page can fit 2 rows of 3 stickers. **Draw 2 rows of 3 stickers.**

Stacia has **6**  stickers.

How many pages does she need? ☐

Shade in this number of pages.

☐ ☐ ☐ ☐ ☐

Book

Stacia has **8**  stickers.

How many pages does she need? [ ]

Shade in this number of pages.

Stacia has **15** stickers and **12** stickers.

How many pages does she need? [ ]

Shade in this number of pages.

How many pages does Stacia need altogether? [ ]

What

Samita took a walk.

She saw 6 cacti. Write two ways to add **equal groups** to get 6. Then make a multiplication sentence.

_3_ + _3_ = 6

____ + ____ + ____ = 6

____ × ____ = 6

She saw 12 cows. Write two ways to add **equal groups** to get 12.

____ + ____ = 12

____ + ____ + ____ + ____ = 12

____ × ____ = 12

3 + 4 are *not* equal groups. There are 3 in the first group and 4 in the second group.
20 + 20 *are* equal groups. There are 20 in both groups!

Samita Saw

She saw 16 sharks.

Write two ways to add **equal groups** to get 16.

_____ + _____ = 16

_____ + _____ + _____ + _____ = 16

_____ × _____ = 16

She saw 8 ducks. Write two ways to add **equal groups** to get 8.

_____ + _____ = 8

_____ + _____ + _____ + _____ = 8

_____ × _____ = 8

Multiplication

Times Table Machine

The times table machine is broken! Fill in the missing numbers to fix it.

×	0	1	2	3	4	5	6	7	8	9
0	0	0	0	0	0		0	0	0	
1	0	1	2	3		5	6	7		
2	0	2	4		8		12	14		18
3	0	3		9		15	18		24	
4	0		8		16		24	28		36
5	0	5	10		20		30	35	40	
6	0	6	12	18	24	30				
7	0		14			35	42		56	63
8	0	8	16		32		48	56		
9	0	9		27	36		54	63	72	

196

You fixed the times table machine! Now you can travel through time and space.

Time travel is cold. Pack 6 bags of socks. Put 8 socks in each bag. How many socks will you bring?

_____ × _____ = _____ socks

Time travel can be dry. Bring 4 crates of water. Each crate holds 4 bottles of water. How many bottles will you bring?

_____ × _____ = _____ bottles of water

Time travel makes you hungry. Pack 4 lunchboxes. Each lunchbox holds 6 food packets. How many food packets will you bring?

_____ × _____ = _____ food packets

Multiplication

Multiplication isn't magic! It just takes practice. **Solve these problems!**

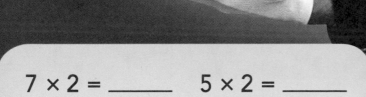

Math-Acadabra!

$7 \times 2 =$ _____ $5 \times 2 =$ _____

$4 \times 6 =$ _____ $1 \times 10 =$ _____

$3 \times 7 =$ _____ $3 \times 3 =$ _____

$2 \times 9 =$ _____ $8 \times 4 =$ _____

$5 \times 7 =$ _____ $6 \times 9 =$ _____

Turn these addition problems into multiplication problems.

7 + 7   __7__ × __2__ = _____

4 + 4 + 4 + 4 + 4 + 4   _____ × _____ = _____

5 + 5   _____ × _____ = _____

3 + 3 + 3 + 3 + 3 + 3 + 3   _____ × _____ = _____

8 + 8 + 8 + 8 + 8   _____ × _____ = _____

1 + 1 + 1 + 1 + 1 + 1 + 1 + 1   _____ × _____ = _____

2 + 2 + 2 + 2 + 2 + 2 + 2 + 2 + 2   _____ × _____ = _____

7 + 7 + 7 + 7 + 7   _____ × _____ = _____

9 + 9   _____ × _____ = _____

6 + 6 + 6 + 6 + 6 + 6 + 6   _____ × _____ = _____

Crack the Code

Each pattern is the combination to a lock.
Complete each pattern to open the lock.

5	☐	15	☐	25	30
2	☐	☐	8	☐	12
6	12	18	☐	30	☐
☐	20	24	☐	32	36

Mimi and Miller multiplied by two. They made some mistakes. Circle them. Then write the correct sentence.

TWO x TWO

7 × 2 = 14

_____

5 × 2 = 7

_____

4 × 2 = 6

_____

2 × 2 = 4

_____

6 × 2 = 8

_____

3 × 2 = 6

_____

8 × 2 = 10

_____

9 × 2 = 11

_____

Hop to it!

Some numbers hopped off the page.
Write them back in!

× 5 = 10

5 × 5 =

4 × ⬚ = 20

6 × 5 =

8 × ⬚ = 40

× 5 = 15

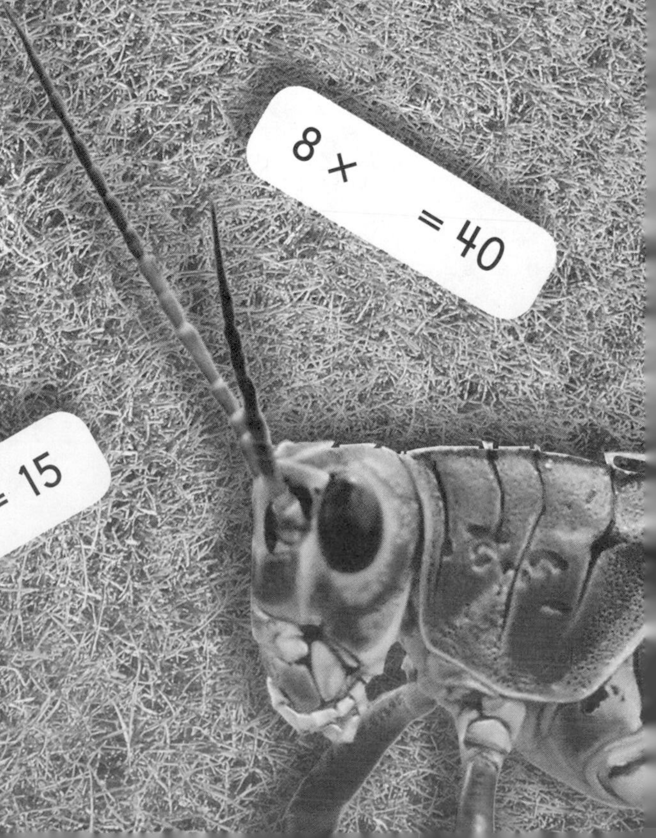

Measurement
and
Data

Measure UP!

Cut a piece of string to match your height. Compare the length of the string to objects in your home.

Draw a star on objects that are longer than the string.

door

pillow

table

lamp

window

sister

What else in your home is longer than the string?

_____   _____   _____

Pinky Ruler

Trace your pinky finger.
Write if each vegetable is **longer** or **shorter** than your pinky.

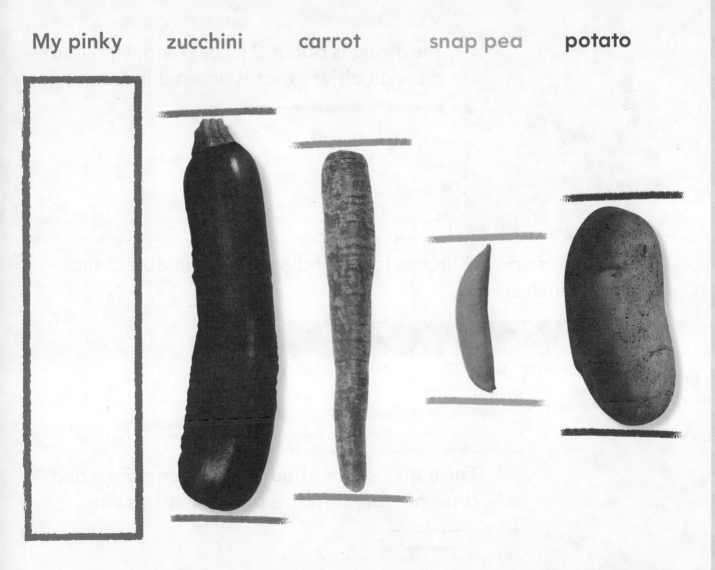

My pinky   **zucchini**   **carrot**   **snap pea**   **potato**

Yo Ho! HUNT FOR MEASURE!

Use each picture to estimate the length of objects in your home.

The string is about 2 inches long. Find and draw an object that is about 3 inches long.

The crayon is about 4 inches long. Find and draw an object that is about 7 inches long.

Blue

The paper clip is about an inch long. Find and draw an object that is about 5 inches long.

Geeta's school supply box is **5 inches** long.

Measure each item. Then circle supplies that will fit in the box.

SCHOOL Tools

Green

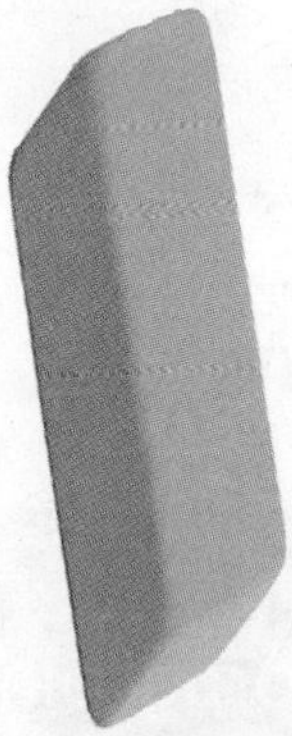

_____ inches

_____ inches

_____ inches

_____ inches

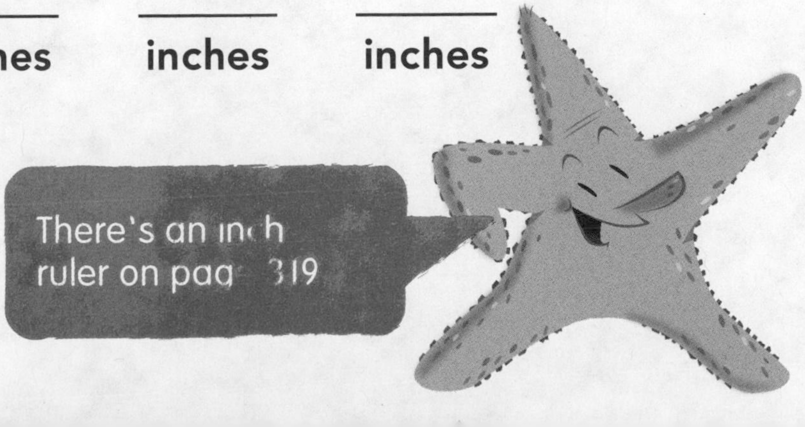

_____ inches

There's an inch ruler on page 319

Bat Dinner

It's nighttime.

The hungry bats leave their caves.

Which bat flies farther?

Craggy Peak

Oak Hollow

Sycamore

Deerview

_____ **centimeters**   _____ **centimeters**

Use a ruler to measure from point to point.

Write the total distance to the nearest centimeter.

There's a centimeter
ruler on page 320.

How **TALL** Am I?

A giraffe is about 18 feet tall.

Stand against a wall.

Put a piece of tape on the wall to mark the top of your head.

Measure from the floor to the tape.

A chipmunk is about 6 inches tall.

This is me.

I am _____ feet _____ inches tall.

I am almost as tall as a chipmunk!

Chop-Chop, Rabbit!

Rabbit makes a salad for his friends.

He needs **3 centimeters** of a carrot.
Measure from the line. Draw a cut line.

He needs **6 centimeters** of celery.
Draw a cut line.

There's a centimeter ruler on page 320.

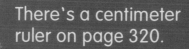

He needs **5 centimeters** of corn.

Draw a cut line.

He needs **3 centimeters** of a jalapeño.

Draw a cut line.

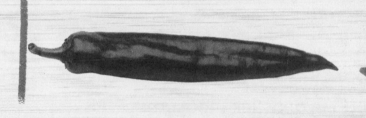

He needs **2 centimeters** of a bean.

Draw a cut line.

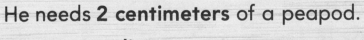

He needs **2 centimeters** of a peapod.

Draw a cut line.

TOOLS
of the Trade

What can you use to measure these objects?
Draw a line to the best tool.

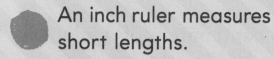 An inch ruler measures short lengths.

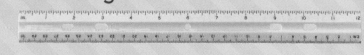

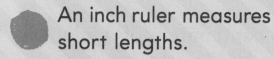 A yardstick measures greater lengths.

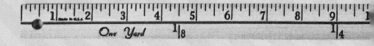

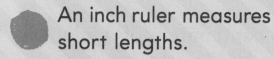 A measuring tape measures things that are not flat.

212

A LENGTHY RIDDLE

Find an object that fits each clue.
Then measure it in inches, feet, or yards.

Find it.	Draw it.	Measure it.
I am longer than 6 inches but shorter than 1 foot.		_____ inches | feet | yards
I am longer than 1 foot but shorter than 1 yard.		_____ inches | feet | yards
I am longer than 1 yard.		_____ inches | feet | yards

A Fishy Job

Jo is a fishmonger. She sells fish. Sometimes she tosses one in the air!

Find the weight of each fish in ounces and in pounds.

	Weight in Ounces	Weight in Pounds
trout	16 ounces	1 pound
salmon	_____ ounces	1 pound
tuna	_____ ounces	10 pounds
monkfish	48 ounces	_____ pounds
flounder	32 ounces	_____ pounds

1 pound is 16 ounces. I weighed 1 pound before the holidays. Then I gained 4 ounces. Now I weigh 20 ounces. *Sigh.*

FLAN-TASTIC

Costa wants to make flan.

The recipe shows kilograms.

Costa's scale measures grams.

Change each measurement from kilograms to grams.

Chocolate Flan

Cocoa powder	1 kilogram	1,000 grams
Sugar	2 kilograms	_____ grams
Milk	5 kilograms	_____ grams
Eggs	7 kilograms	_____ grams
Butter	9 kilograms	_____ grams

1 kilogram is 1,000 grams. 2 kilograms are 1,000 plus 1,000 grams.

Marcus Cooks

Marcus makes a three-course meal.

Marcus makes tea. Add 2 quarts of water to the pot. How many cups are in 2 quarts? Circle them.

Marcus makes pasta. Add 3 quarts of water to the pot. How many cups are in 3 quarts? Circle them.

Marcus makes corn. Add 6 quarts of water to the pot. Circle how many cups are in 6 quarts.

1 quart is 4 cups.

EXPERIMENT-AL

Al filled the beakers with liquid.
Write how many milliliters are in each beaker.

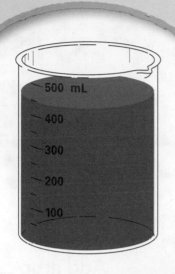

_____ milliliters

_____ milliliters

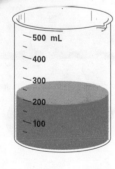

_____ milliliters

<u>350</u> milliliters

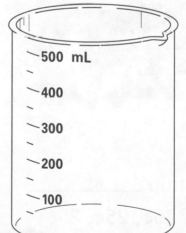

Fill up the last beaker
to 350 milliliters.

Shade it in.

My beaker is always half-full.
That's the kind of guy I am.

Perla's Presents

Perla has $1. She wants to buy candy for her mom.

Add it up _____

25¢, 15¢, 25¢, 15¢, 25¢

Add it up _____

10¢, 15¢, 75¢

Add it up _____

50¢, 75¢, 25¢, 25¢

Add it up _____

25¢, 15¢, 10¢, 50¢,

Draw a heart box around the candy she can buy.

MYSTERY CIN

Draw the missing coin!

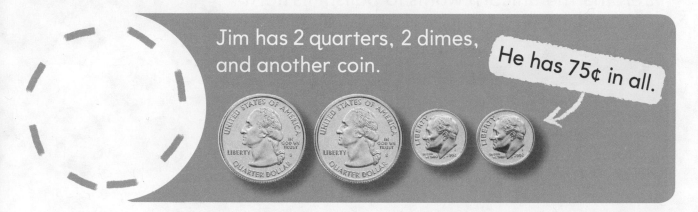

Jim has 2 quarters, 2 dimes, and another coin.

He has 75¢ in all.

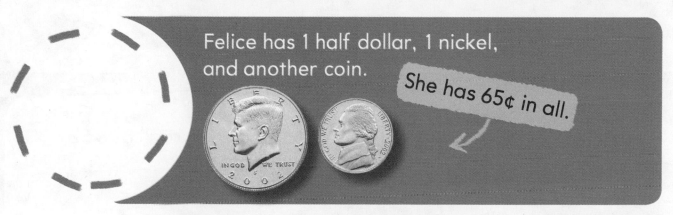

Felice has 1 half dollar, 1 nickel, and another coin.

She has 65¢ in all.

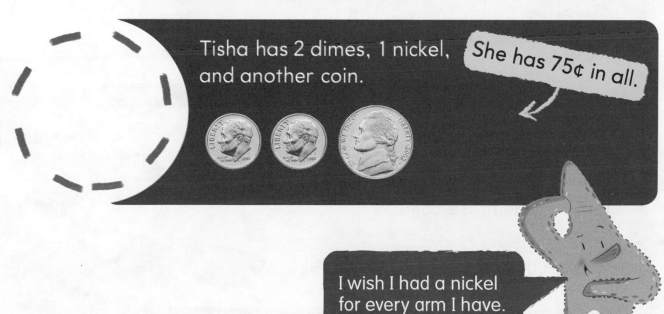

Tisha has 2 dimes, 1 nickel, and another coin.

She has 75¢ in all.

I wish I had a nickel for every arm I have.

Horn POLISH

Jerome the unicorn wants to polish his horn.

Horn polish costs $1.

Jerome has these coins.

Jerome needs _____ ¢ more.

A good cleaning rag costs $2.

Jerome has these coins.

Jerome needs _____ ¢ more.

A Unicorn Horn Brush is $1.50.

Jerome has these coins.

Jerome needs _____ ¢ more.

Cuckoo's Clock

This cuckoo tells time in riddles. Read each riddle.
Draw the time on the clock.

The hour is an odd number.

It is after 1:00.

It is before 5:00.

Cuckoo!

The time is

_____.

It is half past an hour.

The hour is an even number.

It is between 6 and 10.

Cuckoo!

The time is

_____.

The hour is before 8:00.

It is after 4:00.

It is even, if you're keeping score.

Cuckoo!

The time is

_____.

It is half past an hour.

The hour is an odd number.

The hour is between 7 and 11.

Cuckoo!

The time is

_____.

Beatrix had a busy morning. Draw the time each thing happened.

She woke up
at 7:30.

She walked the dog
at 8:00.

She ate breakfast
at 8:30.

She rushed to the
toy store.

It opened at 10:00.

At 10:30 she found
the perfect toy.

Please gift wrap it!

The party starts at
11:00.

Time Twins

Kali and Lacy are twins. Kali has a digital watch. Lacy's watch has a face. Make their watches match.

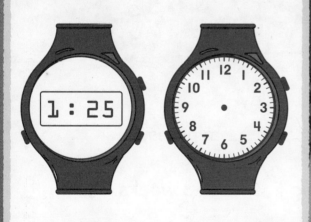

PYRAMID PIZZA

Boy Tut works at Pyramid Pizza.

> There are 60 minutes in 1 hour.
>
> There are 24 hours in 1 day.
>
> There are 7 days in 1 week.
>
> There are about 4 weeks in a month.
>
> There are 12 months in 1 year.

Boy Tut works for 2 hours on Thursday.

2 hours is the same as _____ minutes.

Boy Tut will get his camel-driving license in 3 weeks.
Then he can deliver pizza.

3 weeks is the same as _____ days.

Pyramid Pizza was closed for 4 days.

4 days is the same as _____ hours.

Boy Tut has worked at Pyramid Pizza for 3 years.

3 years is the same as _____ months.

Boy Tut writes the number of hours he worked on a timecard.

1 I	2 II	3 III	4 II II	5 III II	6 III III	7 III III	8 IIII IIII	9 III III III	10 ∩
									100 ⓔ

Monday	I
Tuesday	IIII IIII
Wednesday	II II
Thursday	II
Friday	
Saturday	
Sunday	

Boy Tut worked 5 hours on Saturday.
Write 5 on the timecard in hieroglyphs.

How many hours did Boy Tut work on Monday, Wednesday, and Saturday combined?
Write the sum in hieroglyphs. _____

GROWL and Groove

Gabby loves to dance with her monster friends.
She makes a chart of their favorite moves.
Count the tally marks. Write the total.

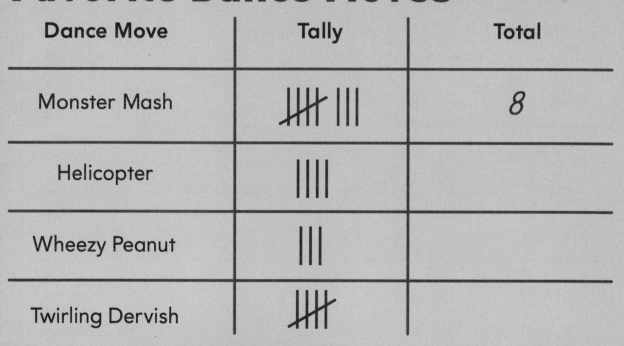

Favorite Dance Moves

Dance Move	Tally	Total
Monster Mash	卌 |||	8
Helicopter	||||	
Wheezy Peanut	|||	
Twirling Dervish	卌	

What is the most popular dance move? _____

How many monsters chose the Helicopter? _____

Which dance move was the least popular? _____

Can you do the Wheezy Peanut? _____

Geometry

Shapes for Less

Marlo shops for shapes. Can you find everything on her list?

Draw a line to the matching shape.

I need:
- sphere
- cone
- cylinder
- rectangular prism
- cube

Delicious
ORANGE
Soft drink

Vitamin C Added

Stack 'Em

sphere   rectangular prism   cylinder   cube   cone

This is a _____.
Can you stack it?   **yes**   **no**

This is a _____.
Can you stack it?   **yes**   **no**

This is a _____.
Can you stack it?   **yes**   **no**

This is a _____.
Can you stack it?   **yes**   **no**

This is a _____.
Can you stack it?   **yes**   **no**

A **face** is a flat side of a three-dimensional shape. A cube has 6 faces. If you ask me, one face is plenty.

ROBOT Body Shop

Help assemble the robot. **Draw a line from the** set of shapes **to the finished** robot part.

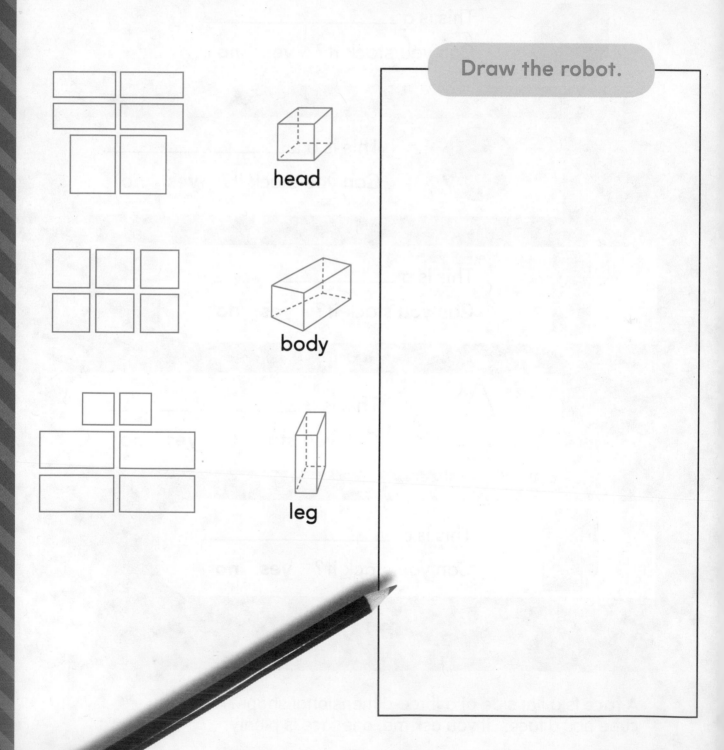

head

body

leg

Draw the robot.

BUILD a HOUSE

1. Add a triangle for a roof.
2. Add two hexagons for windows.
3. Add a quadrilateral for a door.
4. Add a pentagon next to the house. This is a pool!
5. Add a quadrilateral to the pool. This is a diving board!

A **quadrilateral** has 4 sides. A **pentagon** has 5 sides. A **hexagon** has 6 sides. A **hectagon** has 100 sides. Try drawing that!

Mirror Gallery

The gallery lost half of each artwork.
Draw the missing half so that both sides match.

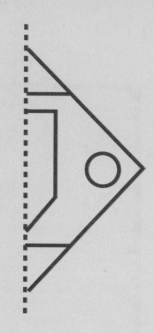

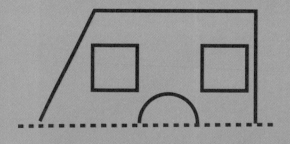

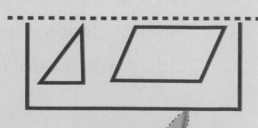

The dashed line is a **line of symmetry**. If you fold on the line, everything will match up. Draw a line of symmetry on me!

Field Day

Marcy makes a pattern with the field day equipment. Draw the next set in the pattern.

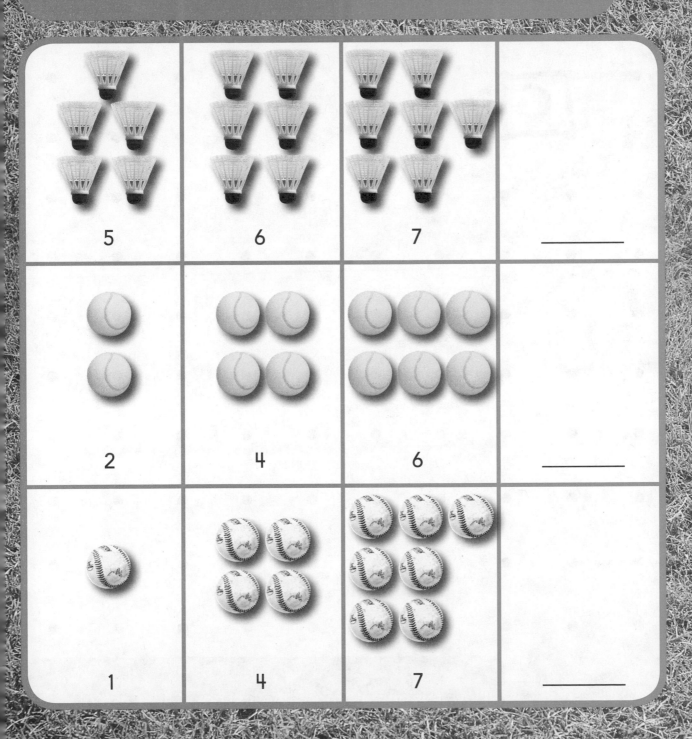

5   6   7   _____

2   4   6   _____

1   4   7   _____

DOTS AND BOXES!

Grab a friend! Play dots and boxes.

Take turns. Draw one line. Then let the other person draw one line.

Try to make a box. If you make a box, it is yours! Write your initial inside. Can you make more boxes than your friend?

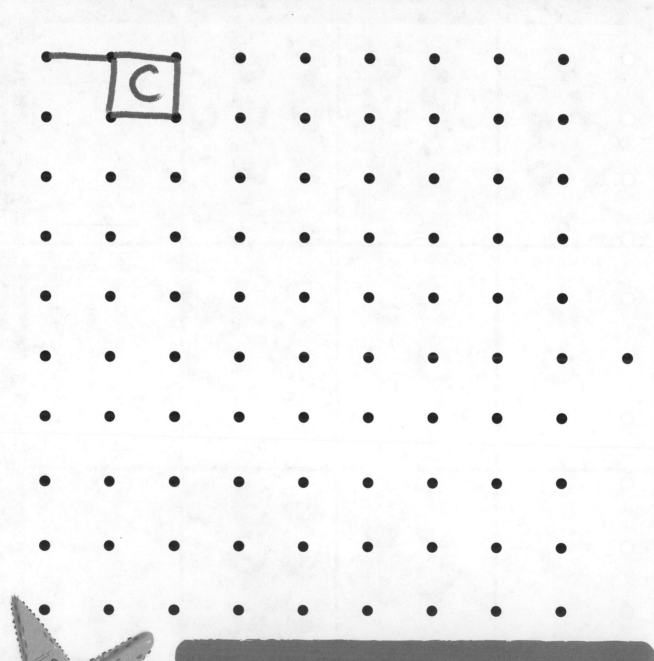

I love this game! I made the first box. C for Cosmo!

Jack, Brie, and Colby

Three mice have a cheese party.
Draw lines to cut each cheese into three equal parts.

The mice serve crackers with **3 angles**. Circle them.

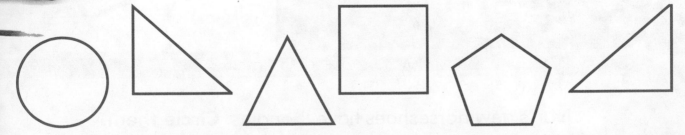

An **angle** is where two sides meet. I have 10 angles.
Circle them! Hey, that tickles.

Quarter Horse

Ivan only eats hay that is cut into four equal parts. **Circle hay for Ivan.**

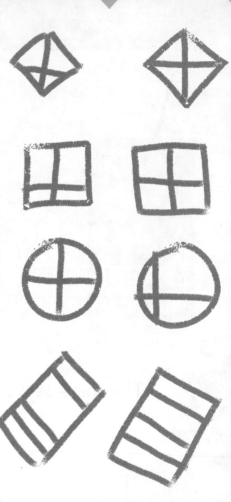

Ivan's new horseshoes have 4 angles. **Circle them.**

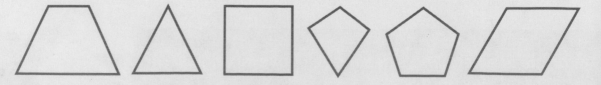

Nature
of
Science

Look and Learn!

You can learn about something just by looking at it. **Write** how many legs **each creature has.**

_____

_____

_____

_____

_____

What do you **observe** when you look at me? I have five arms. Some people call them "rays." Just don't call me Ray.

A Neat Fold

Many things in nature have two halves that look the same. They are **symmetrical**.

Circle them.

Go back to the ones you circled. **Draw a line between the two halves.** That's a line of symmetry.

NAME THE
TOOL

Match each tool to its picture.

tape measure

balance

thermometer

measuring cup

magnifying glass

Circle the best tool to measure a ball.

Franz Makes

Fruit Salad

Guess the length of each fruit. Then measure it. Did you make a good guess?

It is about...	It measures...
_____ inches	_____ inches
_____ inches	_____ inches
_____ inches	_____ inches

1 inch   2 inches   3 inches   4 inches   5 inches   6 inches

A MASSIVE Apple!

Read each sentence.

Draw a line to the object described.

It has **more mass** than an apple.

It has **less mass** than an apple.

It has the **same mass** as an apple.

Mass is the amount of matter in something. On Earth, things with more mass weigh more. In space, a whale and a snail weigh the same—0 pounds!

PUMP UP THE VOLUME

Volume is the amount of space that something takes up.

1 quart = **2 pints** = **4 cups**

Write the total volume.

1  + 2 = _____ cups

1 + 2 = _____ pints

1 + 2 = _____ quart

Circle the volume that is greater.

6  or 1

1 or 3

2 or 2

Poor Noor

Noor loves to travel, but he never knows what to pack. **Write the temperature shown. Then circle the colder temperature.**

_____° Fahrenheit

_____° Fahrenheit

Color the thermometer to match the degrees. Then circle the warmer temperature.

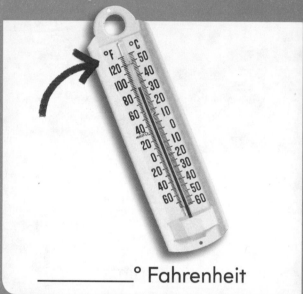

−10° Fahrenheit

20° Fahrenheit

A thermometer measures temperature in units called **degrees**.

PROBLEM

Solved!

A good invention solves a problem.
What problems did these solve?

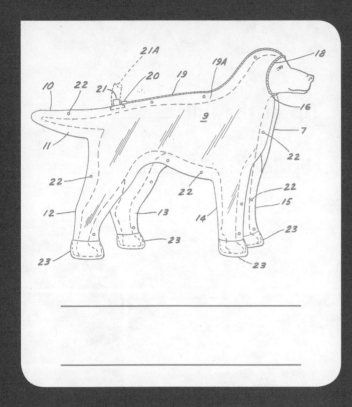

_____

_____

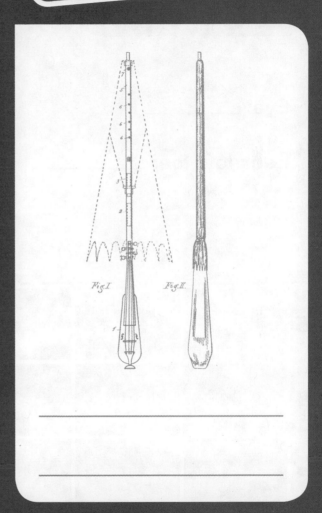

_____

_____

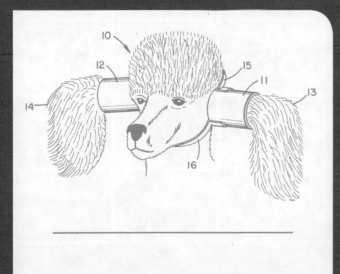

_____

_____

Do you know
another word for
inventor? **Engineer**.

Fossil Finder

Scientists can use a grid to mark where they found things. Write the location of each part.

Eye: __F6__

Tip of the tail: _____

Rear left toe: _____

Hip joint: _____

DRIVING FORWARD

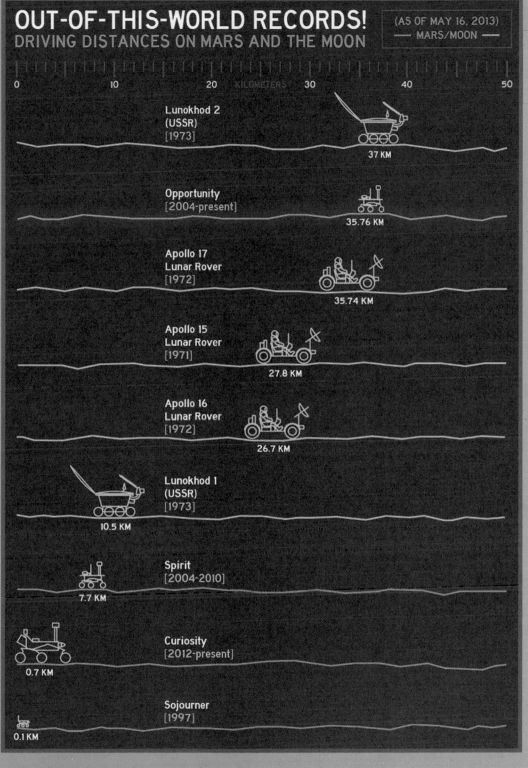

OUT-OF-THIS-WORLD RECORDS!
DRIVING DISTANCES ON MARS AND THE MOON

(AS OF MAY 16, 2013)
— MARS/MOON —

A chart can tell us a lot.

0   10   20   KILOMETERS   30   40   50

Lunokhod 2 (USSR) [1973] — 37 KM

Opportunity [2004-present] — 35.76 KM

Apollo 17 Lunar Rover [1972] — 35.74 KM

Apollo 15 Lunar Rover [1971] — 27.8 KM

Apollo 16 Lunar Rover [1972] — 26.7 KM

Lunokhod 1 (USSR) [1973] — 10.5 KM

Spirit [2004-2010] — 7.7 KM

Curiosity [2012-present] — 0.7 KM

Sojourner [1997] — 0.1 KM

NASA/JPL-Caltech

Which vehicle drove the shortest distance? _____

Which vehicle drove the longest distance? _____

Which vehicle drove 7.7 km? _____

Which vehicle made its trek in 1971? _____

Think Like a Scientist

Esme wants to be a scientist. She uses her inquiry skills to find out information.

Draw a line from each inquiry skill to its meaning.

plan an investigation

classify

predict

make a model

to make a good guess about what will happen

to follow steps to answer a question

to show what something is like or how it works

to sort things by how they are alike

Life
Science

Name That Creature

Fill in the blank. Then draw a line to an animal in that group.

amphibian   bird   fish   insect   mammal   reptile

A _____ has feathers.

A _____ has hair or fur.

A _____ has dry skin covered with scales.

An _____ has smooth, wet skin.

A _____ lives in water and has fins.

An _____ has six legs.

The Weird Parts

Animal parts may look weird. But they can help an animal move, eat, or stay safe.

Draw a line from each sentence to the animal body part it describes.

Wings help me fly.

Fins help me swim.

Suction cups help me climb.

A hard shell keeps me safe.

You have weird parts. Thumbs! What do your thumbs help you do?

_____

Guess who else has suction cups? Me! I use them to grab shells and pry them open.

Do You NEED

Circle things that animals need to stay alive.
Cross out things they don't need.

shelter

water

entertainment

TOYS to LIVE?

oxygen

food

chairs

Reserved for Fluffy

toys

Scientists found evidence that Mars once had fresh water. That means that Mars may have supported living things!

Apartment "BEE"

A shelter, or home, keeps animals safe. Draw a shelter for Buzz the bee.

Now draw a shelter for Tilda the fish. Leave her space to go *swish swish*!

Even fish like to have a roof over their heads. Some fish in coral reefs hang out under *table coral*.

Growing up Green

This frog changed a lot.

Number the steps of his life cycle in the correct order.

froglet

egg

frog

tadpole

Do you know this one? *Why is the frog so happy?* Because he eats whatever bugs him!

Just Like MOM

Many baby animals look like their parents. They are the same shape, just smaller.

Some young animals do *not* look like their parents. Match the baby to its parent.

Do you look like your parents? How?

_____

_____

A newborn sea star is the same shape and color as its mother. Sea star moms snuggle their young. This is called *brooding*. To *brood* means to *protect*.

All You Need Is LOVE ... (and Food ... and Sun)

Don't forget to water the plants! Don't forget to feed the fish!

Plants and animals have some of the same needs. Other needs are different. **Fill in the chart.**

Needs

food	nutrients from soil	oxygen
shelter	water	sunlight

Plants   Both   Animals

FLY FOR YOUR LIFE!

Plants eat too!

Most make their own food. Their leaves can make food out of sun, water and air. Their leaves are tiny food factories.

What part of a plant is like a food factory? Circle it. Then write it.

_____

What does a plant make food out of?

_____

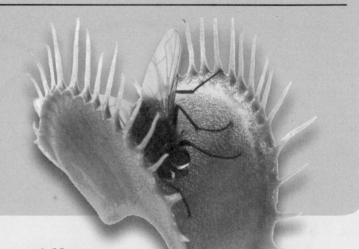

One plant is different. The **Venus Fly Trap** uses its leaves to trap spiders or flies. Then it eats them!

Another plant uses flies. But not to eat! It uses them to **reproduce**, or make more of itself.

The **carrion flower** stinks! It smells like rotting meat. But *flies*? Flies love the smell. So they rush to the flower. They land on it. When they leave, they carry pollen to the next plant. Soon, another carrion flower grows.

What are 2 ways a plant can use flies?

_____

_____

What does the carrion flower smell like?

_____

What would you name a flower that smells like rotting meat? Name it, then draw it.

_____

Pee-ew. Here are other plants you don't want to give your mom on Mother's Day — skunk cabbage, stinkhorn mushrooms, stink lilies, and dead horse lilies.

Traveler's Tale

Plants grow from seeds. But how do seeds get there in the first place?

Seeds can float across the ocean. They can stick to fur or clothing. Some get tossed on the side of the road!

Draw a line from the seed to the way it travels.

You Scratch My Back, I'll Scratch Your...Leaf

Find two ways **plants help animals**. Draw a star.
Find two ways **animals help plants**. Draw a heart.

They spread pollen.

They provide food.

They give shelter.

They move seeds.

Fitting IN

Who fits in? Draw a line.

Brr. It's cold here. A _____ 's thick layer of fat keeps it warm.

It's dry and sandy here. A _____'s long eyelashes keep sand out of its eyes.

It's very dry here. A _____'s thick stem helps it store water.

It's wet here. A _____'s large leaves help it collect falling water.

Plants and animals protect themselves.
Explain how.

This cactus has delicious, juicy fruit. But who would eat it?

The sweet purple pear is covered with _____.

A katydid loves to eat leaves. It also *looks* like a _____ !

This way, other animals can't see it. If they can't see it, they can't eat it!

Think twice before you sneak up on a skunk.

It can _____ you. Then you'll smell bad!

Rabbits won't eat daffodils. They don't taste _____!

Leftovers Again?

A **fossil** is what's left from a plant or animal that lived long ago. Circle the **animal fossils**. Draw a square around **plant fossils**.

Hint: Some are not fossils.

A **fossil** can be a footprint. It can also be bones that turned into rock.

Chain It!

Hawks eat green snakes.

A food chain shows how energy moves from plants to animals.

Draw arrows to show how this food chain works.

Green snakes eat grasshoppers.

Grasshoppers eat grass.

Energy from the sun helps plants grow.

I'm in a food chain.
Clam → Cosmo → *Shark!*

266

Earth Science

CHANGING EARTH

Earth is always changing. Use these words to label the pictures.

earthquake   drought

flood   volcano

_____

_____

_____

_____

It's Natural!

Write three things that come from each natural resource.

bread	pasta	shoebox
cereal	pencil	t-shirt
paper	sheets	towel

wood

cotton

Can you name another natural resource? Here's a hint: You drink it every day.

wheat

Here's Looking at Lunch

Whether you had a ham hero or a radish wrap, the food came from somewhere.

Name the resource used to make it. A resource can be a plant or animal.

My Lunch

What I Ate and Drank	Where It Came From

Orange Juice

100%

Cosmo

Bad Weather

Some weather is so bad, you just want to hide. Now the bad weather is hiding from you!

```
G M S B N U U J B D K Z
C G O E L U D Q D F C Q
N Y N X V B R R D L E Q
G I U I C E A Z E O N R
L B P J N Z R P E O A W
Y X N K Z T Z E D D C B
I W S I X J H H C Z I V
B N L V C A Y G Y Y R J
H B V R G V Z Y I I R Z
T O R N A D O P G L U B
C T L R W V O Y Q A H V
M R O T S R E D N U H T
```

blizzard
flood
hurricane
lightning
severe
tornado
thunderstorm

Some words may be backwards!

There's a storm brewing on this page. What kind is it?

_____

Weather for Feathers

Cecil loves to visit weather around the world. Describe each picture using weather words.

warm and sunny	stormy
hot and humid	windy
rainy	cold and snowy

_____

_____

Know Your CLOUDS

Draw a on clouds you might see on a sunny day.

Cumulus clouds are white and puffy.

They usually mean sunny weather.

Cirrus clouds are thin and wispy.

They usually mean sunny weather.

Stratus clouds are gray and flat.

They may bring rain or snow.

Cumulonimbus clouds are tall and puffy.

They are thunderstorm clouds.

Name these clouds. Then draw lightning bolts on the thunderstorm cloud.

_____   _____   _____

Look outside. What kind of clouds do you see? Draw them.

I see _____ clouds.

Fiery OR Not?

A **star** is a huge ball of hot gases.

It gives off light and heat.

It looks like it is made of fire!

A **planet** is a large ball of rock or gas.

It moves around the sun.

Planets made of gas do not look fiery.

Circle the planets.

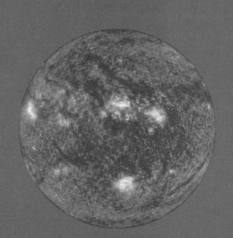

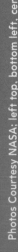

Mercury is the closest planet to the sun. Earth is third. If you want to chill out, go to Neptune. It's farthest from the sun.

Photos Courtesy NASA: left top, bottom left, center.

Sunrise, Sunset

It looks like the sun moves. It doesn't. **Earth is turning!** In the day, we are facing the sun. At night, we are no longer facing the sun.

Where is the sun? **Draw it.**

Is it here?   Or here?

It takes 24 hours **for Earth to make** one complete **turn.**

This is Paola. Where will she be in 12 hours? **Draw her.**

Far Out!

Your mission is to explore our solar system.
Complete your report.

Mars

Earth

Venus

sun

Mercury

Artist Rendering Courtesy NASA/JPL

Uranus

Neptune

Saturn

Jupiter

ACHIEVE

Report by Commander_____

The _____ is a star. The planets move around it.

There are _____ planets.

The planet closest to the sun is _____.

Earth is the _____ planet from the sun.

_____ is the largest planet in our solar system.

The planet that takes the longest time to orbit the sun is

_____.

Pretty Patterns

We see the sun in the daytime. But we have to wait until night to see most stars. Some of them make a pattern, or a **constellation.**

Write the name of each constellation.

Orion
"The hunter"

Ursa Major
"The great bear"

Cassiopeia
"The queen's chair"

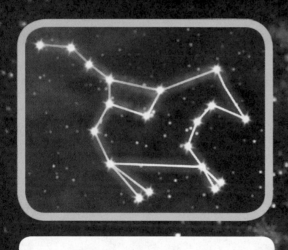

_____

_____

_____

Ursa Major has a group of seven stars called the Big Dipper. **Circle them.**

Physical Science

Polly's Property

Polly brings toys to the beach. Draw a line from each **property** to the matching toy.

- yellow
- bumpy
- big and green
- small and green

A **property** describes what something is like. My properties are: star-shaped, prickly, and adorable.

What **property** does each pair share?

shape   color   texture

_____

_____

_____

THE Shape OF Matter

Match each **property** to its **matter**.

It holds its shape.

It takes the shape
of its container.

It fills all the space
in its container.

gas

solid

liquid

This balloon is made up
of two types of matter.
Circle them.

This glass of juice is made
up of two types of matter.
Circle them.

| solid | liquid | gas |

| solid | liquid | gas |

HEAT IT! COOL IT!

Draw what the matter will look like after it is **heated** or **cooled**.

Heat it!

Cool it!

Heat it!

You can melt an ice cube to make water. Then you can freeze the water to make ice cubes! Unless you have a party to go to, you can do this all day long.

GOOD Vibrations

Sound is made when an object vibrates. To vibrate is to shake back and forth.

quiet sounds = weak vibrations

loud sounds = strong vibrations

Draw squiggly lines to show the vibrations for each sound.

talking

barking

alarm ringing

whispering

drumming

How ATTRACTIVE!

Marty the magnet is very attractive. But only to iron and steel. Circle things that are attracted to Marty.

A magnet can move something without touching it. That's because there's a **magnetic field** around the magnet.

Community

Amelia, Model Citizen

Underline the things Amelia does to be a good citizen.

Amelia woke up early. She decided to spend the day being a good citizen.

She helped her sister get dressed for school. Then she ran to catch the bus.

At school, Amelia was careful to follow the rules. She raised her hand in class when she had a question. "May I go to the bathroom, please?" The teacher was impressed. Amelia was so polite!

At lunchtime, Amelia sat down next to Nancy. Nancy was upset. She forgot to pack her lunch. "Don't worry," said Amelia. "You can share mine."

After school, Amelia saw a neighbor carrying groceries. Amelia offered to carry them.

What a great day, thought Amelia.

Is Amelia is a good citizen? Explain your answer.

_____

_____

Write one way you are a good citizen.

_____

_____

Complete the sentence.

community   citizen

Amelia is a _____ in her _____.

Thanks, Amelia!

People who work and play together live in the same **community**.

Vote for Bubbles!

Ms. Millie's class could not agree on a name for the new bunny. So they voted.

Election Results

Eric	I
Bubbles	II
Mopsy	~~IIII~~
King Henry	~~IIII~~ I

Which name got the most votes? _____

Which name got one vote? _____

How many kids voted? _____

What would you name the bunny? _____

A Tale of Two Kitties

Fluff and Puff live in Phoenix, Arizona. In this desert region, the climate is hot and dry. The kittens' favorite season is winter because the weather is a little cooler.

Fluff's family is moving to the Rocky Mountains in Colorado. In this region, each season is very different. Summers are hot and dry, but winters are cold and snowy. Spring is warmer with lots of rain. In this climate, Fluff's family will wear different clothes in each season.

Which region has about the same climate all year long? _____

Which region has different weather in each season? _____

Would you rather live with Puff in Arizona? Or Fluff in Colorado? Why? _____
_____

A **climate** is the usual kind of weather a place has.

Community

293

Road Trip!

You start a road trip in Tennessee.

First, you pick up a friend in Raleigh.

Raleigh is the state capital of _____.

From Raleigh, you drive north.

You drive over a border into the state of _____.

Virginia is a neighbor to many states. How many?

Virginia shares a border with _____ states.

From Virginia, you decide to visit the national capital.
Circle it on the map.

Draw a line from the national capital to the closest state capital.

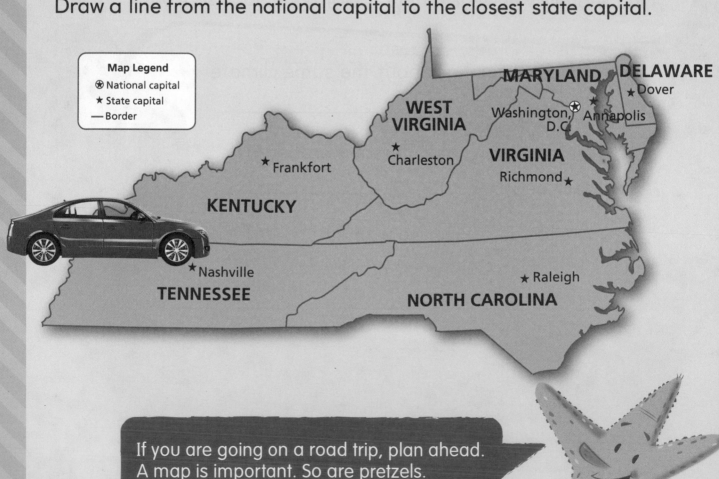

Map Legend
✪ National capital
★ State capital
— Border

MARYLAND   DELAWARE
                 ★ Dover
WEST
VIRGINIA   Washington, ★ Annapolis
                  D.C
              VIRGINIA
★ Charleston   Richmond ★
★ Frankfort

KENTUCKY

★ Nashville
TENNESSEE   ★ Raleigh
              NORTH CAROLINA

If you are going on a road trip, plan ahead.
A map is important. So are pretzels.

Under Foot!

Many maps tell you the names of places.
A **landform** map tells you if the land is
hilly or flat.

A **plain** is a large area of flat land.
There is no uphill. There is no downhill.
Write the names of **two cities** on a **plain**.

_____   _____

A **plateau** (pla-TOH) is high and flat land.
It has steep sides. It can look like a flat-topped mountain.
Write the names of **two cities** on a **plateau**.

_____   _____

Draw a dot on the map where you live.

What kind of land is it? _____

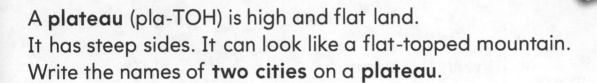

Portland

Boise

Eureka

Sacramento

Monterey

Fresno

Santa Barbara

Long Beach   Los Angeles

San Diego

Phoenix

ROCKY MOUNTAINS

GREAT BASIN

Salt Lake City

GREAT PLAINS

Minneapolis

INTERIOR PLAINS

Chicago

St. Louis

Dallas

Boston

APPALACHIAN MOUNTAINS

Washington, D.C.

Knoxville   Charlotte

COASTAL PLAIN

Atlanta

Orlando

COASTAL PLAIN

New Orleans

Map Legend

- • City
- ~~ River
- ▪ Mountains
- ▪ Hills
- ▪ Plateaus
- ▪ Plains

Small

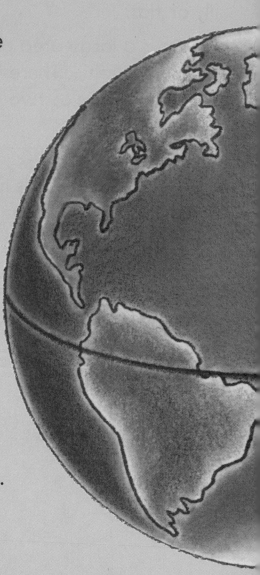

Complete each sentence with the words shown. Then draw a line from the words to the picture.

North Pole

South Pole

equator

Northern Hemisphere

Southern Hemisphere

The _____ is an imaginary line that divides Earth in half.

The top half is called the

_____.

The bottom half is called the

_____.

The _____ is the farthest you can travel north from the equator.

The _____ is the farthest you can travel south from the equator.

World

Draw an arrow to the hemisphere you live in.

Did you know that the hemispheres have opposite seasons? When it is winter in the Northern Hemisphere, it is _____ in the Southern Hemisphere.

Regions near the equator are very hot. Regions near the poles are very cold. I live in the middle. Where it's *just right*.

297

Taxi and Tractor

Sal drives a taxi in the city, an **urban** area.

Carl drives a tractor in the country, a **rural** area.

Are you more likely to find these things near Sal or Carl? **Make two lists.**

apartment building	museums	farm
barn	offices	cornfield
cows	forest	restaurants
windmill	many people	traffic

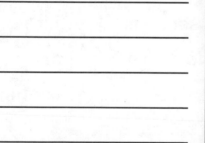

Urban

_____
_____
_____
_____
_____
_____

Rural

_____
_____
_____
_____
_____
_____

The FIFTY-FIRST State

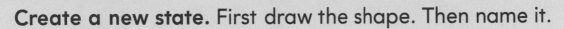

Create a new state. First draw the shape. Then name it.

State name: _____

Circle the resources in your state.

water   **land**   **trees**   **fuel**

Name **three products** that your state can make with these resources.

_____   _____   _____

Name **three workers** that can make these products. What are their jobs?

_____   _____   _____

The ocean is a resource for food and travel.
A **shipwright** can build and repair ships.

A Beary Nice Tree!

The Grizzly Family

_____

Grandfather Max

Grandmother Pilar

_____

Angelo

_____

Ryan

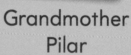
I am not in the Grizzly family. But I like to visit them.

What is the name of this family tree? _____

What is the name of Angelo's father? _____

Who is the youngest bear? _____

Marla's son is Ryan. Add her name to the tree.

Angelo's mother is Grandmother Anna. Add her name to the tree. Then draw her.

Grandfather Juan is married to Grandmother Pilar. Add his name to the tree. Then draw him. He had a mustache.

Grandmother Pilar wore a flower. Draw her.

Grandfather Max wore a hat. Draw him.

How many cubs do Angelo and Marla have?

Draw your family tree! Ask an adult in your family for help.

Treasure Box

People treasure their culture. **Draw an object that tells about your** culture.

I drew _____ to tell about my culture

because _____

_____.

Food, clothes, art, music, and beliefs are part of a **culture**.

Marketplace

GORILLA Whisperer

Willa is a pet sitter for gorillas.
The graph shows how many hours she works each day.

Willa's Hours

	0	1	2	3	4	5	6
Monday							
Tuesday							
Wednesday							
Thursday							
Friday							

How many hours does Willa work on Tuesday?

_____

On which day does Willa work the most?

_____

On which days does she work the same
number of hours?

_____

304

Willa charges a different amount of money for each job.
Circle the job that earns Willa the most money.

Job	Money Earned
Feed gorilla	$1.00
Brush gorilla	$2.00
Paint gorilla's toenails	$3.00
Scratch gorilla's belly	$2.00

Willa wants to buy termite treats.

How many belly scratches does Willa need to give in order to buy termite treats? _____

Good	Price
Bamboo chips (unsalted)	$3.00
Termite treats	$7.00
Blanket	$4.00
Nail polish	$5.00

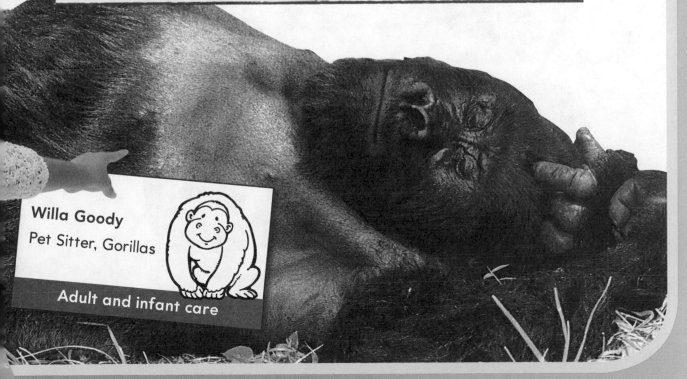

Willa Goody
Pet Sitter, Gorillas

Adult and infant care

GOOD SERVICE

Everyone is at work! Write G next to people creating goods at work. Write S next to people providing services at work.

_____ 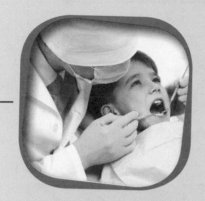 _____

_____  _____

_____  _____

When I grow up, I want to be a doctor to the sea stars. That's a **service**.

Three Kids, Three Countries

Some countries trade products.

Henry, in the United States, goes bananas for oranges!
He eats one every day.
His oranges may come from _____.

Jamie lives in Canada with his mom.
Each weekend, they drive to a mountain park.
Jamie's mom needs a new car.
Her new car may come from _____.

Carlos, in Mexico, helps his dad build a bench.
Now they can sit outside on sunny days. *¡Qué bueno!*
The lumber may come from _____.

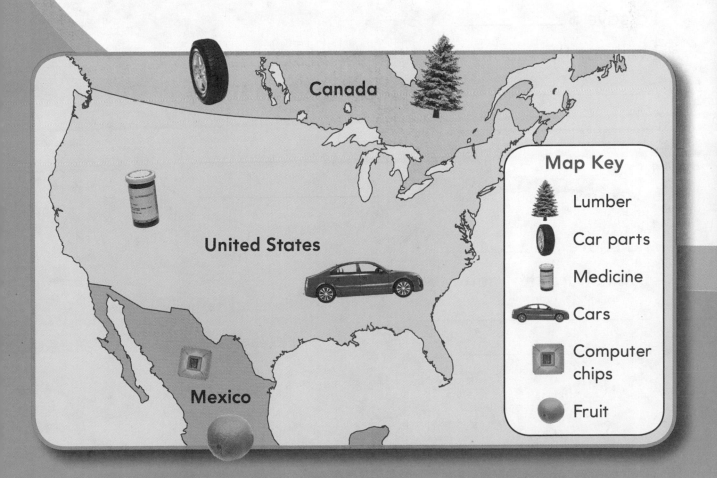

Canada

United States

Mexico

Map Key

Lumber

Car parts

Medicine

Cars

Computer chips

Fruit

A Penny Saved Is . . . Not Enough for a
COMIC BOOK!

Atticus earned $10 for mowing his neighbor's lawn.

His grandmother gave him another $20 for his birthday.

How much money does Atticus have in all? _____

Atticus put $5 in a bank to save up for a new skateboard.

He shared $10 with his library to help buy new books.

He spent $5 on a comic book.

How much does Atticus have left? _____

What would *you* do with $30?

I'd save $ _____
I will put the money in
_____
_____

I'd spend $_____.
I will spend the money on
_____
_____

I'd share $_____.
I will share the money with
_____
_____

You finished the book! Hurry
and go back to page one.
I'm not ready to say goodbye!

Answer Key

PHONICS

p. 8
Sam's words: pen, lot, dip, hat, cup
Kate's words: cube, lime, mole, eve, tape

p. 9
sun/flow/er 3
bas/ket 2
cob/web 2
wa/ter/mel/on 4
nap/kin 2

p. 10
pillow: mice, city, giant, gym
rock: cake, camp, garden, gate

p. 11
frog, plane, swing, grapes, glove, skate, lamp, hand, ring

p. 12
glass, bell, mitt, yellow

p. 13
1. sock
2. duck
3. rock
sock, tent, duck, doll, rock

p. 14
ph to phone
sh to shell
tch to watch
th to thumb
wh to whistle

p. 15
L's over: pilot, later, favor, hotel, tiger

p. 16
Circle: pail, day, may, play, wait, hail
Cross out: car, nose, lime, send, flag

p. 17
queen, beach, eat, peach, tree, bee, feet

p. 18
on long i steps, in any order: find, my, night, pie
on long o steps, in any order: coast, glow, zero

p. 19
dragonfly
centipede
ladybug
spider

p. 20
It's your story — you make up the plot!

p. 21
draw a line from the cart to the party through leotard, shark, art

p. 22
circle horn, ear of corn, shorts

p. 23
water, curb, germ, corner, turn

p. 24
Circle: shirt, stir, swirl, girl
Cross out: tire, dairy, wire

p. 25
underline: pair / pear; weak / week; blew / blue; toe / tow; road / rode; tail / tale; main / mane; rose / rows

p. 26
circle: soft, faucet, lawn, salt, water

p. 27
knot, knock, crumb, climb, gnat, comb, wrap

p. 28
Circle: moon, scoop, soup, group, chew, flew, blue, clue
Cross out: lost, poke, ten, peak, lot, mug

p. 29
Cross out: foot, took, woof, hood, shook, brook

p. 30
clown, flower, house, mouth

p. 31
circle: join, enjoy, ploy, boil, coy, noise

p. 32
needle
window
apple
candle
truck
Draw a line from needle, apple, and candle to the turtle

SPELLING AND VOCABULARY

p. 34
apple, carrots, fish, lettuce, milk, pasta, yams

p. 35
barn, horse, chicken, tractor, cow

p. 36
Circle: take, judge, read, read, done. Line should be drawn from reading to misread.

p. 37
misbehave, mismatch, prepay, misstep, preview

p. 38
overjoyed/very happy; overpay/pay too much; overcrowded/too many people; overdue/past the due date; overuse/use too much

p. 39
circle re; underline fold again
circle un; underline loosen the tie
circle re; underline put the pin in again
circle un; underline open the lock

p. 40
tree
bench
slides
bird
statue

p. 41
windy, quickly, helpful, slowly, dusty, careful

p. 42
kindly, explain, frighten, tasted, rewind

p. 43
soapsuds, folded, steepest, reason, blowing

p. 44
afternoon, playground, sailboat, homework, inside, airport

p. 45

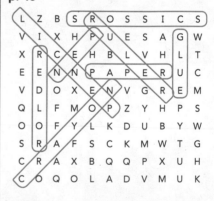

p. 46
Down: 1. flower 2. heard 3. ate 4. write
Across: 5. weather 6. weak 7. rowed 8. deer

p. 47
slip: slide easily, a small piece of paper; present: not absent, a gift; ring: jewelry for a finger, a circle; second: part of a minute, right after the first

p. 48

find and lose
below and above
yell and whisper
fill and empty
weak and strong

p. 49

little / small
glad / happy
brag / boast
baby / infant
tired / sleepy

p. 50

circle: alredy / draw a line to: already
circle: decited / draw a line to: decided
circle: bild / draw a line to: build
circle: bye / draw a line to: by
circle: vist / draw a line to: visit
circle: Than / draw a line to: Then
circle: sprinkels / draw a line to:
sprinkles
circle: forword / draw a line to: forward

p. 51

jobs: doctor, chef, teacher
places: airport, museum, library
tools: hammer, paintbrush, rake

p. 52

photo of orange: juicy, tasty
photo of boulder: hard, gray
photo of guinea pig: small, cuddly
photo of adult and child: helpful, caring

p. 53

hot (scorching) warm

warm, scorching

p. 54

1. cried a lot
2. hurry up
3. understands something well
4. do your best
5. stay cheerful

GRAMMAR AND MECHANICS

pp. 56–57

nouns: ant, girl, song
verbs: pour, sit, walk
adjectives: happy, solid, young
adverbs: boldly, nicely, quietly

p. 58

The bird flew away.
The throne broke.
The princess learns math.
The moat was cold.
Ollie visits the castle.

p. 59

Everyone went inside.
Jane read the book.
The cat woke up.
Tim wore a hat.
The tree fell down.

p. 60

Stan lives in the desert.
~~Pick a small~~
~~Eats insects~~
~~The size of a teacup~~
It burrows in soil.

p. 61

The desert is hot. / statement
Is the desert hot? / question
Find some shade. / command
Stan needs shade now! / exclamation

p. 62

Cara and Kelly fed the cats.
Tara and Tom ate dinner.
Justin and Amelia made the beds.

p. 63

She liked the book.
The horse lives on a farm. / A horse lives
on the farm.
The path goes around a lake. / A path
goes around the lake.

p. 64

Joe: The birds chirped all morning.
Tia likes to read books.
The cat and dog played
together.
Beth: Bill went to the store, and he
bought a shirt.
Everyone ate the apples, but no
one ate the oranges.
We should go inside, or we
might get cold.

p. 65

"I am a majestic creature," says Moose.
"I am majestic, too," says Goose.
Moose asks, "What makes you
majestic?"
Goose says, "I can spread my wings
wide!"
"Hmm. That is majestic," says Moose.
The goose asks, "What can you do with
your wings?"
"These are not wings. These are
antlers," says Moose.
"Oh," says Goose.

p. 66

Nina, Joe, and Suzy went to the park.
They ate hot dogs, popcorn, and
pretzels.
Mom, Dad, Vi, and Rex rode the roller
coaster.
Rex won a goldfish, a ball, and a
unicorn.

p. 67

Sara moved on March 2, 2009.
She moved to Miami, Florida.
Luke got a dog on November 17, 2013.
He got the dog in Cleveland, Ohio.
My grandparents got married on June
23, 1970.
They got married in Phoenix, Arizona.

p. 68

five marbles, two spoons
four cherries, three mugs

p. 69

child/children; man/men; woman/
women; person/people; foot/feet;
goose/geese; tooth/teeth; ox/oxen

p. 70

Past Tense: turned, stayed, jumped
Present Tense: turn, stay, jump
Future Tense: will turn, will stay, will
jump

p. 71

Circle plays, walk, run, listens, puts,
drive

p. 72

Circle: felt, hid, ate, got, drove, said,
broke

p. 73

Subject	Present	Past
I	am	was
You	are	were
He, She, It	is	was
They	are	were

p. 74

capitalize: Poppy, Antarctica, Miami,
Florida, Atlantic Ocean, Dolphins,
Penguins, Tuesday, Pippy, Poppy,
Antarctica, Pippy, Florida

p. 75

Mike's; Omar's; friend's

p. 76

They, It, He

Answer Key

311

p. 77
The book is (yours).
(My) bus is always on time.
(Her) grandparents live in Texas.
The desk is (hers).
That sweater is (mine).
(Your) painting is pretty.
(His) cat is outside.
The folder is (his).

p. 78
January / Jan.; Avenue / Ave.; hour / hr; Street / St.; Monday / Mon.; Road / Rd.; November / Nov.; minute / min.

p. 79
do not
is not
will not
are not
I am
they are
it is
we are

p. 80

READING

p. 82
Sun (draw a picture of the Sun character)
Wind (draw a picture of the Wind character)

p. 83
have a contest / to prove who is stronger

p. 84
1. agreed
2. swift
3. stronger
4. hat

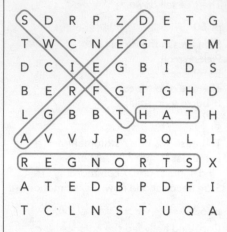

p. 85
shook
flung
tightly

p. 86
Wind wins the contest.
Sample response: Sun smiles because it knows it will win the contest.

p. 87
Circle: He beat down hot and steady.
Circle: The boy took off his hat. The boy opened his coat.
Circle:
(It rains)
(I am hungry)
(I am tired.)

p. 88
Sun bowed.
Sample response: You don't have to use force to get people to do things.

p. 89
3
6
1
2
4
5

p. 90
It needs to be walked.
It can be loud.

p. 91
dogs: need walks, may be loud
both: need brushing
cats: may hide

p. 92
check: Fish do not have paws; Fish do not have hair; Fish can live in bowls.

p. 93
Answers will vary.

p. 95
Mai got Jenny a present because it was Jenny's birthday.
Mai also wrote Jenny a note.

p. 96
Answers will vary.

p. 97
sad; upset; confused
Mai feels this way because she thinks Jenny did not invite her to the party.

p. 98
Jenny wants Mai to be at her party.
Mai thinks she was not invited to the party.

p. 99
paper and a red bow
draw a red bow on the picture of the bird's nest

p. 100
circle the first paragraph
Now they put their notes in a box.

p. 101
Beginning: Mai gets Jenny a birthday present . . .
Middle: Jenny does not visit Mai . . .
End: Jenny and Mai see that the bird . . .

p. 102
sample: This salad has sprouts.

p. 103
circle: look

p. 104
b. She wants people to try to grow sprouts.
You can grow them at home. or Sprouts offer good nutrition.

p. 105
Step 1: the seeds
Step 2: water
Step 3: soak
Step 4: pour
Step 5: twice
Answer will vary.

p. 106
Circle the sentences:
The poet dreamed about sailing the Rio Grande.
The poet dreamed the paper boat ran into a rock.

WRITING

p. 108

Sentence: A walrus is a marine mammal.
Paragraph: A walrus is a marine mammal. Walruses have long tusks . . .
Book: (picture)

p. 109

p. 110

Beginning: Molly was worried. She could not find her cat.
Middle: Molly heard a crackling noise coming from a bag. She looked in the bag.
End: Her cat jumped out of the bag!

p. 111

Answers will vary.

p. 112

See: red
Feel: smooth
Taste: juicy or sweet
Hear: crunchy
Smell: sweet

p. 113

Answers will vary.

p. 114

Answers will vary.

p. 115

Answers will vary.
First, Then, Finally

pp. 116–117

Answers will vary.

p. 118

Both flowers are yellow.
Answers will vary.

p. 119

purple, pink
Answers will vary.

p. 120

They dig the dens out of snow and ice. Their fur helps them stay warm in their cold, snowy homes. Sometimes they build their homes in the middle of a snow bank. Most polar bears dig their dens in the fall. A polar bear's den makes a good home.

p. 121

Mars is an interesting planet.

p. 122

Sample answers: red eyes, brown eyes; small, big

p. 123

These celebrations are all different, but they all honor spring.

p. 124

First, they are big! Second, they can run really fast. They have special claws on their feet that look like hooves. The claws help move their feet. Third, they can hear and see very well. Ostriches are different from other kinds of birds and that makes them more interesting.

p. 125

Answers will vary.

p. 126

We get homework every other night during the week. Why should Friday be different? First, homework helps us remember what we did in class. Second, there is more time for my family to help me on the weekend. We should all ask to have homework over the weekend.

p. 127

the benches are all broken; some of the plastic swings are torn

pp. 128–129

Elephants are the world's biggest land mammals.
An elephant uses its trunk to suck up water.
Elephants use sounds to communicate.
Top idea to bottom picture
Middle idea to top picture
Bottom idea to middle picture.

p. 130

Tornado Alley is the name of an area that has many tornadoes.

p. 131

First, put the glass of water next to your plant.
Next, push one end of the rope into the soil.
Last, put the other end of the rope in the water.

p. 132

p. 133

Answers will vary.

p. 134

Kenya is a country in Africa.
Tell what the climate is like in Kenya.
4
Answers will vary.
Answers will vary.

p. 135

a website about King Tut; a website about birds; a website about how toilet paper is made

p. 136

Lake Superior	Encyclopedia	Great Lakes Facts
Where is it?	Bordered by Michigan, Wisconsin, Minnesota, and Canada	in North America
How big is it?	31,700 square miles of surface area	about the size of Maine
Deepest point?	1,300 feet	1,332 feet

p. 137

Answers will vary.

p. 138

Check the second group.

NUMBERS AND OPERATIONS

p. 140

27, 54, 89, 93

p. 141
Top left ⟶ 150
Second left ⟶ 110
Third left ⟶ 170
Fourth left ⟶ 160
Last left ⟶ 130

p. 142

Number of Sheep	hundreds	tens	ones
437	4	3	7
262	2	6	2
591	5	9	1
814	8	1	4
705	7	0	5

p. 143

Across	Down
1. 323	2. 253
3. 379	4. 923
5. 430	

pp. 144–145
Marisa: 334
Pablo: 245
Tate: 153
Marisa won.

p. 146

	thousands	hundreds	tens	ones
Sasha saw 2,632 stars.	2	6	3	2
Mia saw 1,945 stars.	1	9	4	5
Noah saw 4,163 stars.	4	1	6	3
Jett saw 3,217 stars.	3	2	1	7

P. 147
Noah: $3,247
Jett: $6,410
Mia: $2,958
Sasha: $4,736

p. 148
354: 1 square, 3 lines
253: 1 square, 2 lines
216: 2 squares, 1 circle
314: 1 square, 1 line
264: 1 square
284: 1 square, 5 lines, 9 circles

p. 149
35, 40, 45, 50
70, 75, 80, 85
30, 40, 50
80, 90, 100
400, 500
700, 800, 900

p. 150
Circle 214, 224, 234, 244, 254, 264, 274, 284, 294, 304, 314

p. 151

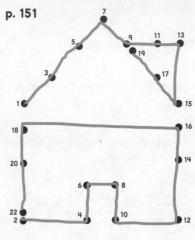

p. 152
321
843
459
921

p. 153
<
=
>
>

p. 154
1. to strawberry
2. to pineapple
3. to banana
4. to mango
5. to peach
6. to cherry

p. 155
220
316
97
158

p. 156
two hundred fifty
ninety-eight
six hundred forty-nine
three hundred seventeen

ADDITION AND SUBTRACTION

p. 158
Bunch 1 ⟶ 8
Bunch 2 ⟶ 7
Bunch 3 ⟶ 5
Bunch 4 ⟶ 9

p. 159
2 + 2 = 4
4 + 4 = 8
6 + 6 = 12

p. 160
11, 10, 9
8, 9, 9
9, 8, 11

p. 161
5
3
3 + 6 + 4 = 13

p. 162
9 + 3 + 4 = 16, 8 + 2 + 5 = 15
6 + 1 + 7 = 14, 4 + 7 + 3 = 14

p. 163
18
6, 8
Draw 13 marbles; Draw Xs over 4 of them.
9

p. 164

1	2	3	4
4	3	2	1
3	1	4	2
2	4	1	3

2	3	1	4
4	1	3	2
3	2	4	1
1	4	2	3

4	3	2	1
2	1	4	3
1	2	3	4
3	4	1	2

2	1	3	4
3	4	1	2
4	3	2	1
1	2	4	3

p. 165

$17 + 4 = 21 \longrightarrow 20 + 1 = 21$
$27 + 6 = 33 \longrightarrow 30 + 3 = 33$
$45 + 6 = 51 \longrightarrow 50 + 1 = 51$
$32 + 9 = 41 \longrightarrow 40 + 1 = 41$
$66 + 7 = 73 \longrightarrow 70 + 3 = 73$
$39 + 5 = 44 \longrightarrow 40 + 4 = 44$
$58 + 9 = 67 \longrightarrow 60 + 7 = 67$

pp. 166–167

$43 + 18 \longrightarrow 41 + 20$
$56 + 27 \longrightarrow 60 + 23$
$32 + 19 \longrightarrow 31 + 20$
$67 + 23 \longrightarrow 70 + 20$
$29 + 29 \longrightarrow 30 + 28$
$58 + 12 \longrightarrow 60 + 10$

pp. 168–169

Barclay
52, 5, 2 draw line $\longrightarrow$ 001
52, 5, 2
Rain
61, 6, 1, draw line $\longrightarrow$ 002
61, 6, 1
Laszlo
73, 7, 3, draw line $\longrightarrow$ 003
73, 7, 3
Bea
60, 6, 0, draw line $\longrightarrow$ 004
60, 6, 0
Cal
84, 8, 4, draw line $\longrightarrow$ 005
84, 8, 4

p. 170

12	–	6	=	6
–				–
8				5
=				=
4	–	3	=	1

8	–	3	=	5
–				–
4				5
=				=
4	–	4	=	0

13	–	5	=	8
–				–
4				3
=				=
9	–	4	=	5

p. 171

$45 + 18 \longrightarrow 63$
$38 + 18 \longrightarrow 56$
$19 + 52 \longrightarrow 71$
$17 + 34 \longrightarrow 51$
$26 + 49 \longrightarrow 75$

p. 172

$39 - 7 = \underline{\ (32)\ }$
$34 - 9 = \underline{\ 25\ }$
$35 - 7 = \underline{\ 28\ }$
$41 - 9 = \underline{\ (32)\ }$
$38 - 8 = \underline{\ (30)\ }$
$52 - 8 = \underline{\ 44\ }$
$38 - 7 = \underline{\ (31)\ }$
$38 - 6 = \underline{\ (32)\ }$
$25 - 8 = \underline{\ 17\ }$
$40 - 8 = \underline{\ (32)\ }$
$37 - 7 = \underline{\ (30)\ }$
$27 - 6 = \underline{\ 21\ }$
$28 - 5 = \underline{\ 23\ }$
$37 - 6 = \underline{\ (31)\ }$

p. 173

13, 5
35, 6
30, 23
54, 62

p. 174

33
38
40
25
65

p. 175

Under B: 24; 17; 39; 43; 38
Under I: 12; 24; 15; 36; 45
Under N: 16; 23; FREE SPACE; 28; 18
Under G: 14; 35; 13; 24; 37
Under O: 26; 25; 41; 29; 24

pp. 176–177

71
67
58
53
46
35
29
17

pp. 178–179

28, 34, 14, 2, 50, 29, 29, 28
MUSHROOM
14, 26, 29, 52
SNOW
50, 16, 18, 40, 50
RIVER

pp. 180–81

16, 8 or 8, 16
15, 5
10, 20
28, 4

pp. 182–183

pink: 534, 85
yellow: 538, 814
green: 518, 418
orange: 216, 167
blue: 438, 471

pp. 184–185

Clockwise from clown: 471, 783, 739, 426, 697, 328, 743, 452, 779, 928

p. 186

4; 9; 5; 3, 1; 2; 8

MULTIPLICATION

p. 188

4 (even), 7 (odd), 12 (even)
3 (odd), 9 (odd), 6 (even)
Drawings will vary.

p. 189

tomatoes:
XXXXX
XXXXX
XXXXX
oranges:
XXX
XXX
XXX
XXX
XXX
XXX
avocados:
XXXXX
XXXXX
XXXXX
XXXXX
XXXXX

pp. 190–191

Drawings will vary.
(odd) (even) (odd) (even)
6 = 3 + 3

pp. 192–193

Drawing:
XXX
XXX
1 page
2 pages
5 pages
8 pages

pp. 194–196
2 + 2 + 2
3 x 2
6 + 6
3 + 3 + 3 + 3
3 x 4
8 + 8
4 + 4 + 4 + 4
4 x 4
4 + 4
2 + 2 + 2 + 2
4 x 2

pp. 196–197
0, 0
4, 8, 9
6, 10, 16
6, 12, 21, 27
4, 12, 20, 32
15, 25, 45
36, 42, 48, 54
7, 21, 28, 49
24, 40, 64, 72
18, 45, 81
6 x 8 = 48
4 x 4 = 16
4 x 6 = 24

pp. 198–199
14, 10
24, 10
21, 9
18, 32
35, 54
7 x 2 = 14
4 x 6 = 24
5 x 2 = 10
3 x 7 = 21
8 x 5 = 40
1 x 8 = 8
2 x 9 = 18
5 x 7 = 35
9 x 2 = 18
6 x 7 = 42

p. 200
10, 20
4, 6, 10
24, 36
16, 28

p. 201
7 x 2 = 14 (correct)
6 x 2 = 8 to 6 x 2 = 12
5 x 2 = 7 to 5 x 2 = 10
3 x 2 = 6 (correct)
4 x 2 = 6 to 4 x 2 = 8
8 x 2 = 10 to 8 x 2 = 16
2 x 2 = 4 (correct)
9 x 2 = 11 to 9 x 2 = 18

p. 202
5 x 5 = 25   4 x 5 = 20
2 x 5 = 10   3 x 5 = 15
6 x 5 = 30   8 x 5 = 40

MEASUREMENT AND DATA

pp. 204–206
Answers will vary.

p. 207
pencil, crayon, eraser, paper clip

p. 208
bat 1: about 12 cm
bat 2: about 15 cm

pp. 209–211
Answers will vary.

p. 212
banana ⟶ measuring tape
sneaker ⟶ inch ruler
glass ⟶ measuring tape
table ⟶ yardstick

p. 213
Answers will vary.

p. 214
16
160
4
2

p. 215
2,000
5,000
7,000
9,000

p. 216
Circle 8 cups for tea.
Circle 12 cups for pasta.
Circle 24 cups for corn.

p. 217
magenta: 450 mL   orange: 400 mL
blue: 200 mL

p. 218
$1.05 $1.00
$1.75 $1.00

p. 219
Jim needs a nickel.
Felice needs a dime.
Tisha needs a half dollar.

p. 220
33 cents
59 cents
54 cents

p. 221
3:00 (small hand on 3, big hand on 12)
8:30 (small hand on 8, big hand on 6)
6:00 (small hand on 6, big hand on 12)
9:30 (small hand on 9, big hand on 6)

p. 222
small hand on 7, big hand on 6
small hand on 8, big hand on 12
small hand on 8, big hand on 6
small hand on 10, big hand on 12
small hand on 10, big hand on 6
small hand on 11, big hand on 12

p. 223
small hand on 1, big hand on 5
small hand on 8, big hand on 1
small hand on 10, big hand on 7
small hand on 6, big hand on 10

p. 224
120 minutes
21 days
96 hours
36 months

p. 225

p. 226
Monster Mash
4
Wheezy Peanut
Heck yeah!

GEOMETRY

p. 228
sphere to yarn
cone to hat
cylinder to toilet paper
rectangular prism to juice
cube to gift box

p. 229
cube; yes
sphere; no
cylinder; yes
cone; no
rectangular prism; yes

p. 230
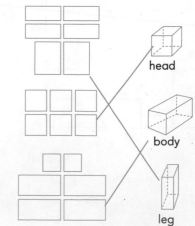

p. 233

8 shuttlecocks
8 tennis balls
10 baseballs

p. 234

Answers will vary

p. 235

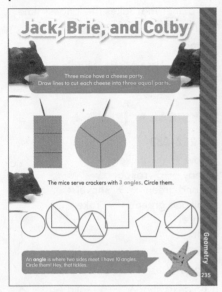

p. 236

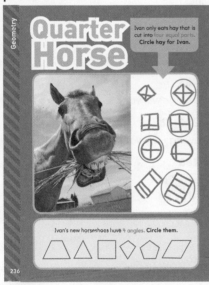

NATURE OF SCIENCE

p. 238

Spider: 8
Dragonfly: 6
Bee: 6
Tapir: 4
Human: 2

p. 239

Circle and draw a line of symmetry down the center of the butterfly and maple leaf.

p. 240

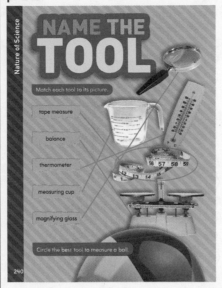

p. 241

Guesses will vary.
Measurements: 2.5 inches; 1 inch; 4 inches

p. 242

more mass: kitten
less mass: dime
same mass: mouse

p. 243

4 cups
2 pints
1 quart
circle 6 cups
circle 3 cups
circle 2 quarts

p. 244

90 /(30)
red drawn to -10 / red drawn to(20)

p. 245

Sample answers: dogs get dirty outside; people want to play music in the rain; some dogs need to protect their ears

p. 246

Tip of the tail: A4
Rear left toe: A1
Hip joint: B5

p. 247

Sojourner
Lunokhod 2
Spirit
Apollo 15

p. 248

plan an investigation ⟶ to follow steps to answer a question
classify ⟶ to sort things by how they are alike
predict ⟶ to make a good guess about what will happen
make a model ⟶ to show what something is like or how it works

LIFE SCIENCE

p. 250

bird
mammal
reptile
amphibian
fish
insect

p. 251

Fins help me swim. ⟶ the fins on the fish
Suction cups help me climb. ⟶ the suction cups at the end of the frog toes
Wings help me fly. ⟶ the wings on the bird
A hard shell keeps me safe. ⟶ the hard shell on the turtle
Answers will vary.

pp. 252–253

Circle water, shelter, oxygen, food.
Cross out entertainment, chairs, toys.

p. 254

Drawings will vary. Bees live in a bee hive and fish live in water.

p. 255

3
1
4
2

p. 256

chick ⟶ chicken
caterpillar ⟶ butterfly
Answers will vary.

p. 257

Plants: nutrients from soil, sunlight
Both: oxygen, water
Animals: food, shelter

pp. 258–259

Leaves should be circled: Leaves sun, water, and air
eat flies / use flies to reproduce
rotting meat
Drawings will vary.

p. 260

apple core ⟶ littering
burr ⟶ sticks to clothing
coconut ⟶ floats across water

p. 261

heart: They spread pollen.
They move seeds.
star: They provide food.
They give shelter.

pp. 262–263

penguin
camel
cactus
plant
spines
leaf
spray
good

pp. 264–265

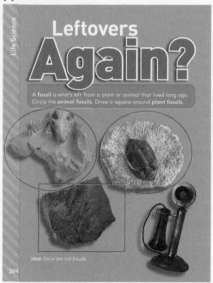

p. 266

grass ⟶ grasshopper ⟶
snake ⟶ hawk

EARTH SCIENCE

p. 268

drought
flood
earthquake
volcano

p. 269

Wood: paper, pencil, shoebox
Cotton: sheets, t-shirt, towel
Wheat: bread, cereal, pasta
Cosmo question: water

p. 270

Answers will vary.

p. 271

a hurricane

pp. 272–273

cold and snowy
warm and sunny
windy
rainy
hot and humid
stormy

pp. 274–275

Draw a sun on top row of clouds.
Cirrus; cumulus; cumulonimbus
Answers will vary.

p. 276

p. 277

Sun should be drawn on left side of page.
Paola should be drawn on the dark side.

pp. 278–279

The sun is a star. The planets move around it.
There are eight planets.
The planet closest to the sun is Mercury.
Earth is the third planet from the sun.
Jupiter is the largest planet in our solar system.
The planet that takes the longest time to orbit the sun is Neptune.

p. 280

Top left is Ursa Major. Middle is Orion. Bottom left is Cassiopeia.

PHYSICAL SCIENCE

pp. 282–283

yellow ⟶ bucket
bumpy ⟶ raspberry
big and green ⟶ shovel
small and green ⟶ rake
texture
color
shape

p. 284

It holds its shape. ⟶ solid
It takes the shape of its container. ⟶ liquid
It fills all of the space in its container. ⟶ gas
solid gas
solid liquid

p. 285

Drawings will vary.

p. 286–287

Drawings will vary.

p. 288

paperclip
safety pin
screw

COMMUNITY

pp. 290–291

She helped her sister get dressed for school.
She raised her hand in class when she had a question.
"Don't worry," said Amelia. "You can share mine."
Amelia offered to carry them.
Answers will vary.
Answers will vary.
citizen, community

p. 292
King Henry
Eric
14
Cosmo!

p. 293
Desert region, Phoenix, Arizona.
Rocky Mountains, Colorado.
Answers will vary.

p. 294
North Carolina
Virginia
5
Washington, D.C.
Line should be drawn between Washington. D.C.
and Annapolis.

p. 295
Answers will vary.

pp. 296–297
equator
Northern Hemisphere
Southern Hemisphere
North Pole
South Pole
Answers will vary.
summer

p. 298
URBAN
apartment building
many people
museums
offices
restaurants
traffic

RURAL
barn
cows
windmill
farm
cornfield
forest

p. 299
Answers will vary.

pp. 300–301
The Grizzly Family
Grandfather Max
Ryan

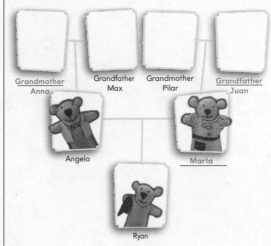

Grandmother Anna   Grandfather Max   Grandmother Pilar   Grandfather Juan

Angelo   Marla

Ryan

①

p. 302
Answers will vary.

MARKETPLACE

pp. 304–305
3
Wednesday
Tuesday and Thursday
Paint gorilla's toenails.
4

p. 306
G: factory worker, farmer, baker
S: Dentist, taxi driver, teacher

p. 307
Mexico
United States
Canada

p. 308
$30
$10
Answers will vary.

Centimeters